Conversations with Screenwriters

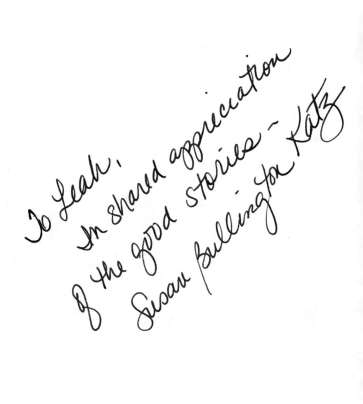

To Leah,
In shared appreciation
of the good stories —
Susan Bullington Katz

Conversations
with Screenwriters

Susan Bullington Katz

with

Ruth Prawer Jhabvala
Frank Darabont
Richard Curtis
Callie Khouri
Mike Leigh
Anthony Minghella
Ron Bass
Horton Foote
Kasi Lemmons
Melissa Mathison
Atom Egoyan
James L. Brooks and Mark Andrus
Sherman Alexie
Stephen Schiff
Neil LaBute
Tim Cahill and Stephen Judson
Roberto Benigni
Marc Norman and Tom Stoppard
David Mamet

HEINEMANN
PORTSMOUTH, NH

This book is dedicated to all writers everywhere
who work in the service of trying to get it right.

And to my children, Eli and Chloe—writers,
adventurers, and good souls.

Heinemann
A division of Reed Elsevier Inc.
361 Hanover Street
Portsmouth, NH 03801–3912
www.heinemann.com

Offices and agents throughout the world

Library of Congress Cataloging-in-Publication Data
Katz, Susan Bullington.
    Conversations with screenwriters / by Susan Bullington Katz.
        p.   cm.
    ISBN 0-325-00295-9
    1. Motion picture authorship.   2. Screenwriters—interviews.   I. Title.

PN1996 .K32 2000
808.2'3—dc21

                                                                    00-033474

Editor: Lisa A. Barnett
Production: Elizabeth Valway
Cover design: Linda Knowles
Manufacturing: Louise Richardson

Printed in the United States of America on acid-free paper
04 03 02 01 00 DA 1 2 3 4 5

Contents

Foreword

Someone once said that a critic is a person who comes onto the battlefield after the war and shoots all the wounded. The person who said that was a writer. Writers know all about wounds.

Susan Bullington Katz knows this, too. Read these interviews with screenwriters and they're bleeding all over the page. With wit and intelligence, to be sure. But bleeding they are, opening up their veins for us. And our good friend Susan's there, cajoling, sympathizing, understanding, getting every last drop out of them.

If you do in-depth conversations with writers in a magazine for writers, you'd better damn well get it right. Susan Bullington Katz gets it right. For five years, every issue of the *Writers Guild Journal* and its successor *Written By* contained a "Conversation with . . ." Susan that was the most readable and stimulating thing in the magazine and invariably the first thing I turned to after taking it out of my mailbox (and looking for a hoped-for residual check).

With a passion for the craft of scriptwriting and detailed knowledge of her subjects' work that borders on spooky, Susan has a knack for posing questions that get the answers we all want to hear. It's so great, when you're struggling with a balky script that refuses to work the way you want it to, to learn that your screenwriting heroes (and only other writers and would-be writers make screenwriters their heroes) regularly face the same nagging fear that you do: that you've been a fraud from the get-go and now the rest of the world (read: "show-biz") will be onto your scam.

While really no moviegoers over twelve really believe the actors make it up as they go along anymore, precious few understand the primacy of the screenwriter in the creative process of making films the way Susan does. The brilliantly-conceived shot or the inspired piece of business that movie reviewers are too quickly inclined to give the director credit for is often to be found on the pages of the screenplay, and Susan ferrets out this shocking information, too.

I personally know several of the screenwriters Susan interviews in this collection. And because she has, in her disarming way, gotten them to reveal themselves so honestly on these pages, I realize that, after reading her conversations with them, I know the others as well. And it will be your pleasure to get to know them, too.

Allan Burns

co-creator, *Mary Tyler Moore*
co-creator, *Rhoda*
co-creator, *Lou Grant*
co-creator, *The Duck Factory*
writer, *Butch and Sundance: The Early Days*
writer, *Just the Way You Are*
writer, *Just Between Friends*
writer, *A Little Romance*

Acknowledgments

Thank you to everyone who encouraged me to do this, from the first friends at that first meeting of the *Writers Guild Journal* Editorial Advisory Board; to Bill Mies, Lisa Chambers, and Tara McCarthy, who edited the magazine during the run; to Ron Tammariello, who did the wonderful graphics and arranged for the photographers; to Mary at the front desk who fielded the phone calls; to Jules Minton, longtime friend and supporter; to Robert Carrington, wherever he is, who urged me not to give up the journalism thing while writing screenplays; to David Ball, whose incredible support at Duke Drama made it possible for me to think I could move to L.A. in the first place, though he will no doubt flinch at the thought of taking credit for that.

A big thank you to my mom, Martha Bullington, and my grandmother, Emmie Cranford, who, every afternoon of every summer of my childhood, when the midday dinner dishes were put away, would sit and rock and tell stories, and who taught me the value of them.

Thanks to my dad, Lee Bullington, who was always telling me things I ought to write about. Like Tom Stoppard, I don't think I've ever written about a one, but the fact that he just naturally assumed I would, or could, was the kind of indicator anyone needs, though I didn't appreciate that till later.

Thanks to Bill Hardy at the University of North Carolina, who gener-
ously gave me his time every Friday morning for a semester to turn that
first play into a screenplay. Thanks to Sam Ragan, who printed my poems
in the Southern Pines *Pilot* and offered me a writing residency at Wey-
mouth at a time I needed it the most. And to his daughter, Talmadge, a
good friend and writer, as well.

Thanks to Sally Buckner, head of the Capital Area Writing Project and
former head of the Peace College Freshman Writing Institute, not just for
her encouragement of me and her hiring of me, but for her encouragement of the many thousands of students who learned directly from her,
and the millions who came to know themselves as writers because of how
their teachers, trained by Sally, encouraged them.

Thanks to my sister, Emmie Gorrell, and to my brother, Lee Bullington, two more of the all-time great appreciators of story. Thanks to Phyl-
lis Murphy for her good sense and help. Thanks to Jeff Sweet, without
whom this book would not exist. Thanks to Susan Schulman, who, as an
agent, took it and me on. Thanks to Lisa Barnett for championing this
project from the start. Thanks to M. J. Kaplan, one of the best interview-
ers, who shared her friendship and enthusiasm for this project and for the
writers herein, and who also hired me so I could afford to live while I was
writing it.

Thanks to all the publicists, producers, and assistants who helped
arrange for these interviews, including Laura Kim, Mark Pogachefsky,
and their colleagues at MPRM; Karen Fried, Tony Angellotti, and their
colleagues at the Angellotti Company; Elizabeth Greenbaum and Nancy
Willen, formerly at Dennis Davidson Associates; the folks at Bumble
Ward and Associates; the folks at Nancy Seltzer and Associates; Fredell
Pogodin; Karen Paul at Miramax; Anna Gross of Checci Gori; and all the
publicists at agencies and studios who help get the stories out.

Thanks to all who watch a movie, or think about going to watch a
movie, and wonder, "Who wrote that?"

And thanks to all the writers I interviewed during that great run in
Written By, who gave their time and insight and didn't balk. I fell in love
with you all, month by month. Thanks to the ones who agreed to be in
this book. Thanks to the ones who aren't in the book. I'm saving you for
next.

Introduction

> The value of life can be measured by how many times your soul has been deeply stirred . . .
>
> —SOICHIRO HONDA

Why do we go to movies anyway? I don't know about you, but I've certainly gone because a certain star was in one, and I wanted to watch him or her on screen for those two hours. Or because it was expected—a Friday night date, a child's birthday party, a Truffaut classic I never saw the first time around. Or because it was Clint Eastwood getting the bad guy—getting the bad guy really good—and it was a day I had just been through my own battles and was real glad to watch him take them on for me and win.

Or it was an opportunity to visit a place I'd never been to, or a place I'd been to and loved. Sometimes it was because I was homesick . . . in a movie theatre in the Netherlands and watching *Gejaagd Door de Wind*, subtitled in Dutch. Or slipping into a theatre in London to watch Dustin Hoffman charge at the church, screaming for Elaine, in *The Graduate*. Or, more recently, watching the North Carolina mountains in *28 Days* in a theatre 2,500 miles away from home.

But of all these, the movies that move me most are the ones that, as Soichiro Honda says, stir my soul.

Think about it:

The scene in Anthony Minghella's *The English Patient* where the Indian bomb defuser hoists a war-worn Canadian nurse into the highest reaches of a bombed-out chapel.

The scene where a teenaged Sarah Polley, one of the few survivors of a horrible schoolbus accident in Atom Egoyan's *The Sweet Hereafter*, decides to lie to save the lives of those remaining in the town and subsequently her own.

The scene where Jack Nicholson's obsessive-compulsive misanthrope and Greg Kinnear's beaten, bruised painter recognize a common point of loneliness between them in Jim Brooks' and Mark Andrus' *As Good as It Gets*.

The scene where Geena Davis' Thelma in Callie Khouri's *Thelma and Louise* calls home to her husband to tell him she's not coming home.

The moment in Horton Foote's *Tender Mercies* where the daughter (Ellen Barkin) finally reconnects with her father and asks him if he remembers the song he used to sing to her, and he says no, and we know it's a lie.

These are the moments that get to us, that catch us up, that make us think and feel and sometimes cry, that make movies worthwhile.

Movies are made of these moments, and there would be none of these moments without the writers.

In the fall of 1995 I was asked to serve on the editorial advisory board of the magazine then known as the *Writers Guild Journal*. At my first meeting, we were all asked to think about what might increase reader satisfaction with the magazine.

"That's easy," I said then, as we pushed back our plates of pasta salads and ham sandwiches. "All we have to do is take out our pens and jot down on our napkins what we'd like to read in the magazine."

I was fairly certain that what I had learned over time applied in this case, too—that I am not that far different from most people, and that what I wanted to see in the magazine would very likely be what others wanted to see too. At the top of my list was "interviews with other writers." And, sure enough, at the top, or close to it, of other people's lists was the same thing: "interviews with other writers."

For where is the writer among us who doesn't want to read about how others do it? To come out from behind our desks and keyboards and find out, after our time in solitary, that others are out there, too, fighting some of the same fights? Some may be fighting bigger fights in terms of scale— hashing out plot points with studio heads or dickering over fees in the seven digits—but, through it all, the biggest fight remains the same: trying to get it right. And then there are the others: once written, how to get it sold? Or how to look at the clock and realize it's three in the afternoon, and not a single new word, much less scene, has been written?

As a poet first, then a journalist, and now a playwright who'd come to L.A. to write screenplays, I wanted to know how my favorite screenwriters did it. The screenwriters who'd stirred my own soul. I'd just interviewed Alan Rudolph for the American Airlines magazine, and I thought it'd be a kick to interview more.

Four years later, I'd interviewed a screenwriter or television writer every month for the pages of the magazine. And what I found out is that there are more common threads among us than disparate ones. That even someone as prolific and as much a household name as Tom Stoppard has doubts about his work. That even Richard Curtis has found himself with a late-afternoon television show on and worried about how little work he's gotten done for the day. That even David Mamet had a time of going to the refrigerator and finding little there.

And mostly, mostly what I found out is a great generosity of spirit among these exceedingly successful screenwriters. Exceedingly successful not just in the box-office receipts for the movies they've written, but in having written moving scripts. And they were all more than willing to sit and talk to me about the work they do, how they do it, and the difficulties they've had with it.

What I learned is that not a one of them thinks it's easy—that the writer's job is easy. They might think it's a great job, or it has its perks or other good things about it, but not a one said, about the actual act of writing, that it's easy.

I learned how Neil LaBute used to write only one-acts because he was afraid that if he stopped before he was through, he wouldn't be able to finish.

I learned how Mark Andrus might have gone to law school, but was fortuitously waylaid, and, while waiting, took a creative writing class which ultimately claimed more of his interest than law.

I learned that it was likewise a fluke that led a teenaged Frank Darabont to Stephen King—he forgot to send the "no, thanks" card back to the Literary Guild in time, and, on his way to mail the book back because he couldn't afford it, he caught a glimpse of a scene in the book he was carrying, *The Shining,* so compelling he had to sit down and read the rest.

I learned how Tom Stoppard has learned to wait and not always have the answers in the beginning—how he stops, listens to what's happening in his plays, and trusts that some essential information will arise as a result.

I learned how Jim Brooks knows the difference between different kinds of laughs and how to elicit them.

I learned how Atom Egoyan sometimes loves the unspoken moments between words more than the words.

I learned how Anthony Minghella read and read and read Michael Ondaatje's book, *The English Patient,* then when he went to write the adaptation, didn't open the book. Not out of contrariness, but out of trust that what was important would rise to the top.

How Sherman Alexie, in the beginning, gave poetry readings to groups of a dozen or fewer.

How Melissa Mathison paid attention when E.T., whom she and Spielberg had agreed would not talk, started to talk.

How Kasi Lemmons created the town of Eve's Bayou in her head and later found out there really was a place in Louisiana created in just the same way.

How Horton Foote held on to the rights to *The Trip to Bountiful* even though he was offered what seemed like reasonable money for it at a time his family needed it, and thirty years later saw the reward from that, as it was made into a movie.

How Marc Norman tried for ten years to get a movie made called *Shakespeare in Love.*

How Ron Bass once wrote a novel then, getting faint praise from a teacher, burned it. With no backup.

I learned that the biggest common thread among all the people interviewed here is perseverance. That even those who feared they couldn't write a second script could, and did. That listening—to oneself, to one's heart, to one's characters—is probably the single key ingredient to getting it right.

And I learned that what I suspected was true in that room at the Writers Guild some years ago is probably true here, too—that I'm not so different. That what I go through to put the words on the page, the push-pull I have every time I sit down at the computer—thrilled to be able to be there, but worried that I may not be able to get exactly what I want to say down on paper or, worse, that I may not have anything worth saying at all—is something that is not unknown to some of our best. I learned that what I both feared and hoped is true might be: that I'm pretty close to normal. And, okay, my perseverance could use some shoring up.

Conversations with Screenwriters

A CONVERSATION WITH . . .

Ruth Prawer Jhabvala

Think quality in screenwriting, and inevitably the name comes up: Ruth Prawer Jhabvala. Oh, you may skitter around the edges of pronouncing it out loud (it's JAHB'-va-la), but she is, yes, the woman who writes the screenplays of those films known under the banner of Merchant/Ivory—with American director James Ivory and Indian-born producer Ismail Merchant. The woman who wrote *A Room with a View, Howards End, The Remains of the Day, Mr. & Mrs. Bridge, Shakespeare Wallah,* and more than a dozen others, including *Jefferson in Paris* and *Surviving Picasso.* Who's won two Best Screenplay Adaptation Oscars (for *A Room with a View* and *Howards End*), been nominated for a third (*The Remains of the Day*), and received the Writers Guild of America (WGA) award (*A Room with a View*) and a MacArthur Foundation grant.

And though her surname is Indian, she encompasses an amalgam of cultures—her life, in fact, the geographic fodder for a Merchant-Ivory-Jhabvala film all its own. German-born and Jewish, she fled as a young child with her family to London in 1939. And, after marrying architect Cyrus Jhabvala, settled in New Delhi. Now she lives in New York, with part of each year spent in India.

In September, she was in L.A. to receive the WGA Foundation Career Achievement Award, and we talked with her then.

SBK: You started to write novels when you were a young mother, yes?

RUTH PRAWER JHABVALA: Yeah, I'd sort of written things before, but I had one small child when I wrote my first novel. And had three by the time I had the third.

SBK: Three children . . .

RPJ: And three novels. At the same time. And I was thirty.

SBK: So here's my very real question: how did you do that?

RPJ: I'll tell you very simply: I was in India, with lots of domestic help.

SBK: Ah ha . . . I read about your writing from ten to one every day. Has it always been that?

RPJ: Well, it used to be ten to one and then again like from three to five or three to six, or something, but now it's only ten to one, yes.

SBK: What do you remember of reading when you were very young? Were you an early reader?

RPJ: I think so, I must have been. I always had books. But I started reading in German. I switched to English at twelve.

SBK: Do you remember some of those books?

RPJ: No, I don't at all, I'm afraid. They were German, but I just don't remember anything about that time at all.

SBK: And then when you were in England from twelve on . . .

RPJ: Oh, lots of things . . . mostly novels. I went through the whole of Dickens when I was about . . . well, this was during the war—twelve, thirteen, fourteen . . . I remember reading *Gone with the Wind* in an air raid shelter . . . that must have been 1940.

SBK: And reading about the destruction of Atlanta at the time your own city . . .

RPJ: And the bombs going over London, yes.

SBK: Were you writing at age twelve?

RPJ: I must have been—I mean, I always remember writing something or other.

SBK: So by the time you were thirty, you had three books and three children, and shortly thereafter you got the infamous call [from James Ivory and Ismail Merchant]. . . .

RPJ: Actually it was four years after. I was just publishing my fifth book at that time, but the one they bought was my fourth book, *The House-holder.* I was thirty-two when I published that, and they came when I was thirty-four.

SBK: And you pretended to be your own mother-in-law?

RPJ: [Laughs.] You know, it gives you time. Somebody says, "Uh, can I speak to Mrs. Jhabvala?" And you say, "Yes . . ." and then you hear what they want, and then, "Oh, you want the *other* Mrs. Jhabvala!" They were strangers calling, and I didn't know what they wanted.

SBK: And did your husband really suggest they might be fly-by-nights?

RPJ: Yes, he suggested that. He said, "You won't see those again." [Laughs.]

SBK: When you adapt books, the books you choose to adapt, they're filled with introspection, and your movies are filled with introspection, and yet they're visual. This is a dilemma for anyone, I think, working outward from the interior. How do you go about interpreting visually this introspection?

RPJ: Well, I just have a very good director. I take a scene and I really don't think much about it, how it's going to be in a film. I just think, "How are these two characters going to interact with each other?" I know it can't be the same as on the page in a novel—it must be much more direct and the language has to be simpler. People ask me what's it like to be a screenwriter. . . . It's the skills you learn as a novelist you just apply to that—

good dialogue, strong scenes, characters interacting with each other, and an overall plot. When people ask me, "How do you start writing a screenplay?" I always tell them, "Why don't you start writing novels first?" You can learn so much when you do it all yourself. . . . And there's no quick and easy way to learn it; you just have to spend years of this to practice. I mean, you have to be basically a writer, but you have to practice, also. Just practice writing fiction, and the films sort of look after themselves. Maybe this only applies to someone like myself, who is basically a writer and not a filmmaker. Others might approach screenwriting from the opposite direction, as it were—from their interest in films. Unlike myself, these screenwriters might sooner or later become directors.

SBK: As you're writing every day, are there times when you go, "Yes! I've got it—I've got that right, now"?

RPJ: No, you don't really know that till sometime later. Sometimes it's not till a couple of years later. . . . *Jefferson in Paris* I wrote in 1989, so I've had five years. . . . I'm usually ready with the screenplay a few years before they are ready to film, so I write several drafts over those years. . . . The only exception to that was *The Remains of the Day*, which had to happen very quickly, and I really didn't have much of a chance to redo that.

SBK: I'd love it if you'd talk a little about the process of adaptation, how you go about adapting a novel.

RPJ: I read the book once, twice, three times. I've read it in the past, usually, but I read it again several times, and then I make an abstract of each scene. Then I put the book aside, and working from my abstract or my synopsis, I turn it around in a way that it would work for a film—compress here, expand there, turn things around. That I do without looking at the book. Then I work from that.

I go from scene to scene, working right through from beginning to end. Then I have a first draft, not as it was in the book, but as I've made—my new construction. Then I rewrite, strengthen some scenes, throw out a lot that I have written, find where it's weak, strengthen that, and so it goes on.

SBK: You said the other night that when you write a script, you send it to James Ivory and he usually sends it back with almost everything crossed out?

RPJ: Well, not almost everything, but he scrawls all over it, usually in red pencil or green pencil—like a school exercise, it comes back to me.

SBK: What kinds of things does he scrawl over it?

RPJ: Oh, "this won't work" and "this sounds absolutely wrong" and things like that.

SBK: Well, I was impressed also with your story about Shakespeare Wallah *and the disagreement that went on for months in correspondence between the two of you.*

RPJ: At that time I was living in India, and he was living in America, and we had lots of time to work, because we didn't have any money at all, so there was really not much chance of making it. So it was all a kind of theoretical exercise, and we could really learn that way. And then somehow Ismail found the money, so we made it. We knew that once we came up with a script that worked, he would find the money, but meanwhile we didn't have any deadlines, no financiers breathing down our neck, nothing. We just had the luxury of going backward and forward. And the mails were very good at that time. I'd write and he'd get the letter in five days, and I'd get his reply in five days . . . so ten days. That was very fast at that time.

SBK: Do you remember what the disagreement was about?

RPJ: He wanted the playboy to be an actor, and I said, "No, no, we've got to have somebody outside that whole setup of actor, because there's another character who's a Bombay film actress, and then there's English actors," so I thought we had to have one character who's not within that, but sort of outside it.

SBK: I wonder if this kind of balancing act, achieving a balance, is something you learned from novel writing.

RPJ: I think so. I've learned everything from that, really. And then I started learning from films, as well. But I think I could not have learned from films if I had not written all these novels and really learned how to set characters in motion. If you just sit down and write a screenplay, I don't think you can.

SBK: Which movies did you learn from as well?

RPJ: All of them, because we'd build them up bit by bit at the script stage, and then I'd come in the editing room and see what's been shot, and then we'd reshuffle, and I'd learn what works in the film. It would work differently than in the book. That I learned in the editing room.

. . . Also I used to write too much dialogue, 'cause that's what you do in a book. You do everything yourself, by dialogue. When it comes to films, you begin to understand that the actors are in fact doing 50 percent of the work for you. You don't have to put in everything—they'll show it with mannerisms and inflections and all sorts of things—it takes a long time to learn.

SBK: In The Remains of the Day *or* Howards End—*a lot of it is in Anthony Hopkins' and Emma Thompson's close-ups. . . .*

RPJ: Yes, yes, exactly. Now in a novel you would write that out—I mean, you would either give that to them in dialogue or you would give it in an interior monologue or you would somehow have to suggest it yourself. Here you have to give them the opportunity to express it in their own way.

SBK: Now I'm really curious as to how that looks on your page when you're finished—your direction to them.

RPJ: I don't give any direction—I mean, an actor doesn't want that sort of thing. They want lines of dialogue that are rich with possibility for them.

SBK: So is your page spare in terms of everything but dialogue?

RPJ: Completely spare. Absolutely.

SBK: When I was listening to James Ivory and Ismail Merchant the other night and you in the same space, their voices seemed to be rather loud.

RPJ: You can say that again! [Laughs.]

SBK: And yours didn't. And yet you were credited with winning arguments, so I wondered how you do that, and what is that art of collaboration, or the art of compromise, with them?

RPJ: We don't really have direct confrontations—like I described with Jim how we could go to and fro with the script. Actually I prefer not to work with somebody sitting next to me, but at some distance. . . . We worked out that way because we were so far apart. . . . If somebody, you know, scribbles all over your script, well, if he were sitting next to you and he was doing that, you'd get furious. But if he passes it on to you, and you have time to think about it, and weigh your arguments, and then make your notes back to him—it's a calmer way of doing things.

SBK: You live in the same building now?

RPJ: Yes, we do. But even if he's upstairs and I'm downstairs, we still do it like that. As you say, as you hear, he's got a much louder voice, so I wouldn't have much of a chance if we were in the same room.

SBK: Who is it that you respect in the moviemaking world or in the writing world apart from your own team?

RPJ: Nowadays? Whose films I like? I like Martin Scorsese a lot. I like Oliver Stone. I like Robert Altman. I like Louis Malle. Well, I like quite a few directors, and they are very different from ourselves.

Martin Scorsese's film—I loved *Goodfellas.* It was so authentic—you knew that, yes, this is the way these characters live, this is the way these characters speak. That's, I suppose, the mark of any good work of fiction or film—it's authentic. Is it the real thing, or is it something that somebody just made up in order to make a film? You know, it just has to spring out of a person's deepest knowledge and feelings.

SBK: What do you think people are responding to in your films?

RPJ: Well, I hope it's what I respond to in other people's films—the authenticity, that we haven't just made this up. I mean, this is something we really wanted to make. We didn't just say, "Oh, let's make a film." These were issues, persons, places, things that we wanted to show. Things that mean something to us. We're not interested in just making a film, or just making some money—we want to make what we think, what has impressed us, what has touched us. And I hope that comes across to audiences. I mean, you be true to yourself, you just hope that others will catch that spark from that.

SBK: You've received lots of accolades. What's something someone has said, either publicly or privately, about you that has made a great impact on you?

RPJ: Well, fortunately or unfortunately, we had many years in the wilderness . . . all our early films were really not successful and we had a very tough time getting each film made, so by the time people actually went to see our films, we got quite old, really. So it didn't mean that much any more. But maybe it's better that way rather than things coming to you when you're young.

A CONVERSATION WITH . . .

Frank Darabont

It's a house once owned by Ginger Rogers. Red-tile roofed, multi-leveled, an easement where coyotes sometimes clamber up in search of kittens. Now mission furniture fills the dining room, and the walls are lined with one-sheets of *War of the Worlds* and *Invasion of the Body Snatchers*. This is the home of Frank Darabont, writer/director of *The Shawshank Redemption* and cowriter of *Mary Shelley's Frankenstein*.

"Lookit all the friends you can have over," he says, pointing to the table. "And a big pot of spaghetti . . ." And he's off, making plans for the new house much like he's made plots for scripts, like *The Fly II*, *Nightmare on Elm Street 3*, eight episodes of *The Young Indiana Jones Chronicles*, and two *Tales from the Crypt* (one of which, "The Ventriloquist's Dummy," was nominated for a Writers Guild Award).

And now he's directed his first feature, as well—one that's been nominated for a Golden Globe as Best Screenplay and garnered a nomination for its costar, Morgan Freeman, as Best Actor.

On a sunny day before Christmas, Frank Darabont sat on his patio in the hills of Los Feliz and talked about the nine years it took to become an "overnight sensation." And of being, at year's end, on two distinct lists: many Ten Best (for *Shawshank*) and some Ten Worst, (for *Mary Shelley's Frankenstein*).

SBK: You started out in '81 as a P.A.?

FRANK DARABONT: '80, actually. That was the year that Lennon was shot, wasn't it? It's funny how you combine jobs you were doing with historical events and get a chronology of your life after a certain point. That was when Lennon was shot, and my very last job crewing as a set dresser was January of 1986—that's when the space shuttle blew up. And I came back to L.A. and suddenly was a writer, after nine years of trying. [Laughs.]

SBK: How did that happen?

FD: Well, I had been writing all throughout that period. I was constantly trying to *(a)* develop my skills and *(b)* get someone to care.

Chuck Russell [director of *The Mask*] was the line producer on that very first movie, in 1980, who hired me as a P.A.

I had written a spec script for *M*A*S*H* which of course went nowhere, but the costume lady was curious to see what I was doing, so she asked me if she could read it. She liked it and slipped it to Chuck behind my back. So after the movie wrapped, I suddenly got a call from Chuck, who was in the early days kind of struggling, too, and he called me and asked if I wanted to write with him.

I soon moved into the art department and started set dressing. What made that particularly good for me was that it allowed me to take a job, make enough money to be able to sit at home for a month, maybe two months, and write. And it would be terrific, because I was never one of these people who could work a job and then go home at night and write—I need to be able to focus on one thing at a time or I'm a mess.

I had a good friend, Greg Melton, who is now a very hot up-and-coming production designer, that I went to high school with. We started together as P.A.s. He very rapidly moved into the art department, and during those years he was art directing, I was his swing leader or set dresser.

SBK: And all this time you were thinking that you wanted to be a writer?

FD: Oh, yeah—I knew that since I was five. Once I saw my very first movie in a theatre, *Robinson Crusoe on Mars,* which my big brother Andy took me to see, and I made him stay through three showings of it, so he got in trouble when we went home 'cause it was after dark, and Mom walloped him, I think. [Laughs.] I've wanted to be a storyteller ever since then, 'cause it was so magical. Of course, at five I didn't know what the hell it meant, exactly. But I did have some vague notion that somewhere there was a storyteller. Where there was a story, there had to be a storyteller, so that's really what I wanted to do.

So there I am, set dressing, and continuing to develop as a writer, and based on a spec that I had written that never got made, I suddenly started getting work.

SBK: What was the spec?

FD: It was called *Black Cat Run*, sort of an action thriller/road chase movie. . . . Then Chuck got a development deal over at New World to do a remake of *The Blob*, so we went in on that together, and it was the first honest-to-God, you-kinda-get-paid-real-money, you know, WGA minimums, and it was great.

And right on the heels of that, the same day we typed "Fade out/The End," Chuck had been in to pitch ideas on *Nightmare on Elm Street 3: Dream Warriors* to New Line, and they decided to offer him the job of directing that. They needed it redone in a big hurry, 'cause they were planning on shooting it in three weeks. So Chuck and I jumped in his car, drove up to Big Bear, rented a cabin, and rewrote the script in eleven days, beginning to end, and three weeks later he was on a set saying, "Action!"

SBK: Were you nearby so you could see him working as director?

FD: I was there minimally, because by then I was on to the next job. I really wanted to get those scripts written before they caught on to me and realized I was a fraud.

But I didn't need that experience by then, because, quite honestly, I'd had that experience as a set dresser. That was film school for me. On any given job I always lobbied to have the set dresser's position, because as a set dresser you're right next to the director, right next to the camera, right next to the DP, watching what they and the actors do, shot by shot, and so I had five years of experience observing. It was the best film school you could ask for.

SBK: What were some of the things you learned during that time that you specifically carried into your current-day directing job?

FD: Oh, Lord. Mostly they exist on a purely pragmatic level, like number one: you're always fighting the clock. You're always compromising something. Although maybe "compromise" isn't necessarily the word one should use. It's more like getting realistic with your resources and your time vs. what you thought you were going to be able to shoot.

And also the knowledge that there is no such thing as being rested. 'Cause it's an incredible forced march. Sometimes it's a forced run.

Have you ever read *The Long Walk* by Stephen King? It's got this Shirley Jackson "Lottery" feel to it—it's in this sort of alternate world that's very much like ours except that every year they have this big event, called the long walk. And young boys, high school boys, are eligible to join the long walk. They start in Maine and see how far south they walk until there's a winner. The catch is you can't stop, you can't fall below a certain speed while you're walking, otherwise you get a warning. And if you get three warnings, the soldiers who are accompanying you shoot you, and they leave you dead. So it's winning by attrition. There's only one winner—and he's the last guy to stay alive. That's what shooting a movie is like—that's what directing is like. [Laughs.]

SBK: *What were some of the realistic accommodations you had to make in shooting* Shawshank?

FD: It usually boils down to knowing how little you need, really, to cut a movie together well, to tell a story well.

Certainly having Roger Deakins as my cinematographer was an enormous help, because we had, I think, a very good collaboration, and he has wonderful visual ideas and a real knack for being able to take five setups and work them into two, or sometimes even one.

So after a while it becomes almost a game. Particularly with a movie like *Shawshank,* the challenge becomes how gracefully can you convey those things visually, and how few setups do you really need to tell the story.

I remember one scene which was the warden's press conference—Bob Gunton standing in front of the prison with the press. I can't remember my shot list exactly, but I think I may have had ten setups slated for that scene, plus I don't know how many extras. And I figured I'd need all kinds of coverage—I mean, you'd want to see the warden, you'd want to see the press, you know, on and on. . . .

My producer kept yanking the scene out of the schedule because she insisted we didn't have time to shoot it. And I kept saying, "Nicki, let's figure out how, because we can't not have the scene." I mean, it's a narrative button, you can't get away with not pushing it.

So I kept trying to pare down the number of setups. Finally I got it down to one setup plus one quick cutaway, and we would have shot it in about an hour flat had it not been for a little trouble with our aerocrane.

We didn't need all the extras—I just kept a few dozen from the extras we'd had that day, tossed them in different clothes—and it's actually one of the shots I'm proudest of 'cause I love the way the camera just sort of floats in over their heads while Morgan is narrating, and it just kind of eases up and reveals Bob Gunton there delivering his address to the press. I love that.

So sometimes what we call compromises are actually opportunities to improve your visual style of storytelling.

SBK: Can you tell me a little bit about adaptation and how you work from the original written page, adapting it into your screenplay?

FD: Well, King's novella is this very amiable sort of narrative that rambles—it's basically Red, the character that Morgan Freeman plays, telling you the story on the page—from a first-person perspective. And it's a treat to read—it's got a real sort of Mark Twain feel to it—but mechanical screen structure it's not! So there was a lot of rendering that narrative into a linear piece of screenwriting.

I guess the best example would be the institutionalization theme in the story. Because it's Red telling you this, "Well, here's what being institutionalized is like." Ay, chihuahua! Now how do you take that idea off the page and illustrate it?

The way I did that was I took the character of Brooks Hatlen, the Jim Whitmore character, and expanded his character in the movie from a brief mention in one paragraph in the novella. Brooks was ten lines in the novella—"I once knew this old guy, Brooks Hatlen, he got out and couldn't make it on the outside"—that was it. So one has to write James Whitmore scenes and a part, and suddenly that becomes the thematic spine for the entire movie. So there was invention, yes.

But I always try to keep in mind what the author intended in terms of character, in terms of theme, before I invent something.

I did the same thing with adapting Mary Shelley's book, which was a thrill. There was a lot of invention there. Of course, her narrative was, what is it, one hundred eighty years old? The storytelling conventions were completely different. They didn't hesitate back then to hang an entire plot on a chain of twelve wild-ass coincidences. And that's a minefield to get through and make those not coincidental, but actually inherent to the narrative. But I always tried to remember what she had in mind when changing stuff.

SBK: When did you read King's novella originally?

FD: When it was first published, which I believe was '82.

I had been a fan of King's since *The Shining* was published. I was in high school, and I never had two nickels to rub together, but I joined the Literary Guild anyway—you know, they'd send you the card saying "We're going to send this to you unless you send the card back to us"—a real sneaky way to get books into people's hands. *The Shining* was their main selection, but I thought, "I can't afford this"—maybe it was like eight bucks back then, but it was a fortune to me. But I forgot to send the card back, so they sent me the book. I opened it up and I looked at it and I said, "Oh, shit, I have to mail it back to them," and as I was moving across the room to put it back in the box, I just happened to open up the book, just out of sheer curiosity, 'cause you can't not open a book when it's in your hands, right?

And it happened to fall open at the end of one of the chapters where the dead woman sits up and grabs the little boy by the throat, and I thought, "Hold on! This ain't going back in the box—this is too interesting!" So I sat down and read it and managed to scrape up the eight bucks somehow to buy the book.

And then a book called *Night Shift* was published—a lot of his short fiction—and I was knocked out by this one story called "The Woman in the Room," which was about a guy whose mother is dying of cancer in a hospital room. And I sat down and wrote a little adaptation of it and sent it off to him with a letter saying, "Dear Mr. King, I'm just a kid, but I sure would like to make this as a short film."

So he granted me permission to do that. This was when I was twenty, I guess, and it took me three years to make that thirty-minute short, which was finally finished at the end of '83. And that year was pretty lean for me, 'cause I think I made something like $11,000 that year, and $7,000 of it went into the movie. Anyway, King was very happy with the final film. We got aired on PBS a few times, and won a few festival awards. . . .

SBK: How much did you offer for the rights to do "Woman in the Room"?

FD: Oh, Lordy—I don't even remember. At the time, though, I was not rolling in dough—I was piss-poor, actually. It must have been a couple hundred bucks, maybe.

Then in '87, five years after *Shawshank* was first published and I first read it, I approached him again for the rights to that because I was looking for material to start my directing career. And Steve said, "Okay."

So we worked out an option arrangement, and it was certainly more than "Woman in the Room," but it was still a real deal for me because this is a very generous man, and by then I guess we'd become friendly and he liked my work.

SBK: More than three figures?

FD: Eh, it was in the four-figure range. [Laughs.]

So I got the rights and didn't do anything with them for five years, for a number of reasons. One thing is my writing career had really kicked in by then, and you just do not want to turn down work when that happens. It takes years to get over the feeling that maybe it's a fluke and they've made a mistake. I think on a certain level, also, I was waiting for my abilities as a writer to catch up with my ambitions for the script. I don't think I could have written it nearly as well when I first optioned it. But the day came when I felt like I was ready to try it. So I sat down and wrote it in eight weeks, and two weeks later we had a deal with Castle Rock.

SBK: Was that the deal for you to direct it?

FD: Yes. We went in with me attached as director, so that was understood from the get-go.

SBK: I remember hearing the scuttlebutt about Frank Darabont holding out to direct. Two weeks hardly sounds like a hold-out.

FD: [Laughs.] No, it wasn't a hold-out from that standpoint. They immediately fell in love with the script and immediately decided they wanted to make the movie, and boom, we made the deal. Then maybe a month later, they kind of came back to the table. I don't know how word got out about this, but everyone has wound up asking me about it, so obviously it wasn't Hollywood's best-kept secret. Rob [Reiner] was looking for his next movie to direct, and was having trouble finding something he could get excited about. And, quite honestly, the script that he had gotten most excited about was mine.

So they, in a very gentlemanly way, said, "Are you sure you want to direct this, because if you would consider selling it, we'll pay you a shit-load of money and give you a pay-or-play deal as writer-director on a project to replace it."

And I thought about it. I had to sleep on it, not just because of the money, but it was Rob Reiner asking. Rob Reiner is a great filmmaker, and I knew that he would make a terrific film, and that gave me pause.

But I said "no," and never another word was said about it. They took "no" for an answer very graciously, and Rob did particularly, and proceeded to be the biggest supporter, biggest booster and mentor and friend to me and to this project that you could imagine.

Which, by the way, if anybody has a great script, I say go straight to Castle Rock with it—you'll never be treated better in your life. You can ask anybody who's worked for them.

SBK: Of course, you realize this is going to cause a run on Castle Rock.

FD: Good! They're expanding their production slate, they need the product! So take it over there, tell 'em Frank sent ya. As for me, boy, if you liked Shawshank, it's because of Castle Rock. Because they trust their filmmakers. And as we know, creative trust is the rarest commodity in this business. Their idea of studio notes is they will tell you what they think, and then they let you make your own decisions. It's a company that was established by filmmakers, and they know what it's like, what the need for trust is.

I once asked George Lucas why he left Hollywood, why he went up and built his own empire, and he said, "I could never get anybody to trust me down there. I got tired of having to fight for every page of what I do." That's why George is up north.

SBK: I saw a screening of Shawshank *at the AMC Century 14—you were there, I remember—and the audience applauded.*

FD: That is the best feeling in the world. I think that's why we do it. Completely why we do it. It's not for the dough. That we get paid is sort of a pleasant by-product. We do it because, I think, or at least I do it, because there's nothing like having an audience applaud at the end. There's nothing like pushing all those buttons as you go through the story and have an audience react the way you decided a year and a half ago they were supposed to react. There's nothing better than surprising them and hearing them gasp, or amusing them and hearing them laugh, or touching them and hearing them sniffle. That is the best.

1995

A CONVERSATION WITH . . .

Richard Curtis

Richard Curtis is on time. It's the Windows Lounge of the Four Seasons, the morning after the Golden Globes, the morning after he hasn't quite won for Best Screenplay for *Four Weddings and a Funeral*. And it's the third straight week of rain, a day that seems less like L.A. and far more like London, which is fitting, because that's where he's from.

And as he drinks tea, he talks of his work and his charity—the British version of Comic Relief, which he and a colleague started nine years ago, and which takes up months of his time each year. And of Emma Freud, the documentary presenter with whom he lives, and the baby they're expecting in June.

SBK: Where in England do you live?

RICHARD CURTIS: I live in the middle of London, in Notting Hill, in a converted Baptist chapel, with a baptism font. . . .

SBK: In your house?

RC: Yes, and I'll give any of your readers $50 if they can think of what to do with a baptism font! I don't really know what to do with it.

SBK: I heard that you had been to more than two or three weddings before writing Four Weddings and a Funeral.

RC: That's right. I went through a whole decade when I went to so many—either '72 or '68, I forget, but an enormous number of Saturdays—gone!—never to be reclaimed. Always with that frantic trying to get there on time, which I never, never managed. I once was four-and-a-half hours late for a wedding in Exeter.

SBK: And what happened?

RC: Well, I turned up during the farewell speeches [laughs], you know—my car crossed paths with the bride and groom as they left.

SBK: So there's a little bit of Charles in you?

RC: Oh, a little bit. I think he's both a fictional character and a combination of various traits of friends and people I know. I do have a close-knit group of friends who did go to a lot of these weddings together, so I suppose I just compiled him.

SBK: Have you ever gone through a wedding of your own yet?

RC: No. I've been best man once. It didn't last. [Laughs.] I don't want to act as a curse on anyone else's, no.

SBK: Were you with Emma all during the writing of this movie?

RC: Yes, absolutely. She is incredibly important to the process. I do think it's the process of writing which is probably more important than the ideas, and she is vital to the process. She script edits like nobody's business.

SBK: In what way?

RC: She tries—because she's the person I'm fondest of, it's in a way her job and easy for her—to find the problems right from the beginning. So I'll say, "This is the story that we're going to do," and she says, "Yeah, yeah, yeah—but, you know, what's it really about?" and stuff like that.

So we talk about things in advance, and then she reads the scripts with a horrifyingly slow speed. It always exasperates me. I give her this script which is meant to be light as air and take an hour and a half to read, and it takes her about six hours. And she has a big red pen and I keep on saying, "You can't be understanding what's meant to be happening—you're going so slowly!" And she marks it all up.

"CDB" is her favorite thing, which stands for "could do better"—"CDB" and big crosses-out and "you must be joking." But she puts some ticks, too. We go through that process ten, fifteen, twenty times. I'm very lucky like that. I think that's an amazing thing, to have someone take that care with you even before it gets to other people.

SBK: So you really do go through twenty drafts.

RC: I don't know that there are people who do many less, actually—but yes. *Four Weddings and a Funeral* didn't in fact change that catastrophically. It was, from the very first, quite close to what it was going to be. But there's a hairline between something that works and doesn't work, so I did lots with Emma, and then a draft for Mike [Newell, the director] to convince him to do it, and drafts for Duncan [Kenworthy], the producer, and all of that.

SBK: How are they all different?

RC: In *Four Weddings,* a lot of the drafts would be to try to give everybody a full story. You know, that first time around one just tries to make the construct work. And I always have to write a lot of jokes just to make me feel secure that there's going to be some jokes in it eventually.

And then Mike and Duncan made me talk through what each character's arc was—so there's a lot of doing that, in each case trying to give somebody a key moment, a real story. One of the things I do is to read the film endless numbers of times pretending I'm the actor who's been given a particular part, and only concentrating on what their feelings would be, and what they hoped would happen next, and what their character would do.

And then there are drafts to solve certain technical problems. I spent a whole month writing one scene—the scene after the funeral, where Charles and James Fleet stand by the river and discuss things. 'Cause there's a kind of logical problem there, which is that the funeral is meant to say something . . . it's the truest moment in it . . . about the nature of true love. And yet the next thing that has to happen is that Charles has to marry the wrong person. So there was something illogical there, and I had to find a way of making him draw the wrong conclusion.

Eventually I did that by putting him with someone with different feelings about it, and yet with tremendous integrity. So that he actually talked to someone at that point who said, "You know, I don't expect a thunderbolt. All I expect is a certain level of contentment and happiness." And therefore it was sort of logical that Charles would come to the wrong conclusion.

That took me ages to work out. That scene used to have lots of other people in it and be about different things. And then it took a long time to figure out who he should almost marry.

SBK: You say you sit down with Emma on January 1 and plan out your year. . . .

RC: Yes, and this January we decided for the next three years. . . . We've got a child up and coming, you see, so we've had to change. . . . I'm not writing the sequel, but I'm living it! [Laughs.]

I tend to work by letting things fester for a long time. The next two things I want to write are things I've been intending to write for years and years and years.

SBK: Can you tell me a little bit about them?

RC: One's about a young bloke falling in love, so that's an easy one, and the other one's about two old people who've always been in love.

SBK: Do I detect a theme running through here?

RC: It's odd, isn't it, really? It's odd that the nature of true love should be of such interest to me, but I suppose so. I don't think of myself as being obsessed by the subject in real life, but it would be extremely boring to write films about somebody who works too hard [laughs], which is probably the thing which has obsessed me more than anything else.

SBK: The chronology that I have for you, that I know about you, begins with Rowan Atkinson.

RC: My mum will be hurt by you saying that, but! . . . [Laughs.] You mean the work chronology, yes, all right.

SBK: So is that true, is that where that began?

RC: Yes, we started writing sort of sketches at university . . . at Oxford. I was a graduate and he was a post-graduate. . . .

SBK: How did you meet him?

RC: At a writers' meeting for a revue. For the first three times I met him I thought he was an interestingly shaped cushion because [laughs] he was so quiet. He never said anything, he just came along because he had an instinct that that was where his talent lay.

And then just at the end of this long process with all of us writing absolutely frightful sketches and reading them out and nobody laughing, Rowan stood up in the fourth meeting and said he had a couple of ideas and did these two brilliant almost mimed sketches where he would speak words and enact them, so "Hello" would be this halo over his head, and it was a startling moment, because they were like nothing you'd ever seen before. . . .

The first thing we did was called *Not the Nine O'Clock News,* a TV sketch show. And then we did a stage show, which I suppose is in some form or another the basis of *The Tall Guy,* the film I did with Jeff [Goldblum].

SBK: And then you went on and did Black Adder *together?*

RC: Yes. Very much the same team as *Not the Nine O'Clock News*—the same producer, Rowan, and me. Then I wrote the second series of that with a guy called Ben Elton, who's a fabulous writer.

SBK: When you were writing Mr. Bean, *were you writing alone at home?*

RC: *Mr. Bean* is the strangest thing. There are no words. And it works best, I think, when there isn't huge technical crockery. What happens is you've got Mr. Bean in an extremely simple comprehensible situation, and then he messes things up or finds extraordinary ways of making himself comfortable.

So I do it by standing in my room at home in front of a mirror. The only way to do it is to act it out. And then we take it in to Rowan and he makes it funny.

SBK: So if anybody were to look in the window . . .

RC: They would think I was insane in slow motion. I remember it took hours and hours to work out one where Rowan was in a royal lineup, waiting for the Queen Mother to come, and it was all about him practicing his handshake and practicing his bow. They would have thought I had some tragic repetitive syndrome where I kind of frantically had to re-enact this handshake.

SBK: You mentioned that when you were a kid, you put cotton in your jowls for the Godfather *effect. Did you think you might be an actor?*

RC: As an actor, I'd obviously peaked when I was fourteen in a school production of *A Winter's Tale* when I played Hermione, the tragic misused wife . . . so the only way I could get on stage at university was writing stuff for myself.

I turned out to be very bad at acting.

In fact, if you watch it, I'm in *The Tall Guy* giving an astoundingly inaccurate and weak performance playing Man Coming Out of Toilet. In an extremely unconvincing orange moustache. I'm coming out of the toilet when Jeff's going in, and I sort of nod to him, which I've been told never happens. This is a horrible bit of acting, because it's quite true—you never meet the eye of people when you're passing in that circumstance.

So even the tiny role I had, I blew.

The bottom half of my legs were in the first cut of *Four Weddings*. I played Man in Kilt. Then I got cut, too, out of that.

SBK: Did you have Hugh Grant in mind when you were writing the part of Charles?

RC: We didn't have anyone in mind. And God bless him, when Hugh came, he was just ideal—every word, every line he said was right. He understood Charles entirely . . . and he found it easy to be extremely accurate in comic delivery, with the rhythm of the jokes, while having the right character.

SBK: I wanted to ask you about that beginning scene. I know you did many drafts, but did it always start out with that scene that went on for seven minutes with just one word?

RC: Yes. I think so. We used to say that since we didn't have the money to start with a car chase or lots of explosions, we only had the explosive nature of the English language to go on, so that was our special effect.

When the movie opened, I tried to engineer it that my mother arrived late.

It's funny. I know the Queen of England has seen the film and enjoyed it, so I've got a feeling that often when people object to what is called bad language, I think it's because the bad language is an expression of hatred and hostility, and it's not that in our film. It's an expression of panic and chaos and sweetness, really. And I think that's why people don't really mind it.

SBK: What is your day like?

RC: Oh, horrible. Horrible! Horrible to behold. Shameful in every way. [Laughs.] I always claim to be so hardworking, but I'm sure I'm just the worst in the world.

I get up at about ten, have a cup of coffee, read a newspaper, and have a little doze 'cause I'm worn out by that time. At 11 o'clock make some phone calls till around twelve when the first of the news programs comes on television. Have lunch, watch *Neighbours,* which is an Australian soap opera, watch about ten minutes of *Sesame Street,* then say, "Oh, God, I can't be watching *Sesame Street,* surely!," make a few more phone calls, then at about 3 o'clock think, "Oh, this is so disgraceful. I must get to work."

Then I sit down and write until the point where I write one thing I think is good, then celebrate by taking about an hour off. Sometimes I even start celebrating before I've committed the good thought to paper, and then I come back from the celebration and can't remember what it is I was celebrating. And then just work very, very late into the night . . . while watching a lot of television.

SBK: So after supper you really get rolling.

RC: Now that we're going to have a child, I'm thinking of genuinely becoming one of those proper writers who, you know, goes to the shed in the garden and works from ten till twelve and then has lunch and works from two till six. We'll have to see whether or not I can do that.

SBK: Do you have the shed out back?

RC: We don't have the shed, no! That's maybe what the baptism font will be used for.

A Conversation with . . .

Callie Khouri

Some of the things you've heard about are true. She did live in a log cabin for part of her growing-up. She did start out as an actress. *Thelma and Louise* was, truly, her very first script. Ever.

And it garnered her an Academy Award for Best Original Screenplay (only one of three females to earn one for a solo credit), a Writers Guild Best Original Screenplay, and a Golden Globe Best Screenplay. And it set the path for the four years it would take her to write the next one.

Three days before her second film, *Something to Talk About,* was due to open, Callie Khouri sat in Mani's Bakery in Santa Monica and talked about writing her sophomore script and more.

SBK: I've read a fair amount about Thelma and Louise, *but what I don't know is how it came into being.*

CALLIE KHOURI: I had been working for years with Amanda and Julian Temple. We did a lot of music videos and stuff, and we had worked together in production for years. I asked Amanda, when I finished *Thelma and Louise,* if she wanted to produce it with me for me to direct. And we started shopping the script around a little bit at that point.

She gave it to Mimi Polk who was working with Ridley [Scott] just to get ideas on which low-budget companies might be interested in doing a movie like this. Mimi read it and said she'd like to show it to Ridley, and that's how it got made.

SBK: So originally you were planning to direct it?

CK: Yes.

SBK: How long did it take you to write it?

CK: Six months. I wasn't encumbered by any expectations.

SBK: Well, that was my next question.

CK: Well, it was daunting. It was pretty much like saying, "Gee, I think I want to go surf" and catching a tsunami on your first wave. But it was really exhilarating, it was really fun, and I think I kept it as much in perspective as I possibly could under the circumstances. But nonetheless, it's a huge life-changing experience to go, as I always jokingly say, from total obscurity to relative obscurity overnight.

SBK: As you were writing Thelma and Louise, *were you producing music videos during the day and writing by night?*

CK: Yes. Or on days that I didn't work. I was freelance, so a job would take anywhere from two weeks to a month, and you'd have a few down days. . . .

SBK: Both Thelma and Louise *and* Something to Talk About *started with you and made it all the way through the process without being rewritten by anybody else, yeah?*

CK: Yes. I was fortunate enough to be working with producers that just didn't believe that calling in another writer to rewrite it would have been the right thing to do. But I also made the choice to work with them, as opposed to a million other people I could have worked with.

SBK: How did you choose Paula Weinstein and Anthea Sylbert [to produce Something to Talk About*]?*

CK: We just met and started talking, and I thought they were great. They had tremendous respect for what a writer does. They gave me tremendous freedom. They were patient almost to a fault—I mean, it did take me four years, and they never pushed me.

SBK: What was it that took you so long?

CK: First of all, it was just that thing with posing yourself the problem of telling a story that's completely character driven, that doesn't have guns and car chases and outward plot things to drive the story. It all has to be driven emotionally. And so you have to find those emotional cataclysms, and it's gotta be real.

And it's not like you can write the end first. Everything is built upon the thing that directly precedes it. So you have to write it chronologically, even though you have an idea—I knew I wanted to have the Charity League scene, I knew I wanted to have the poisoning . . . but you have to write it the logical way that it would happen in terms of its emotional through-line.

And I was so distracted after *Thelma and Louise*—I'd never written anything before that, I had no idea anything like that could even possibly happen. So I just, you know, dealt with that. I also got married, and . . .

SBK: During those four years?

CK: I got married in 1990. *Thelma and Louise* started shooting, I got married, and bought a house all in one two-week period. So I had gone through a big life change anyway. And then, you know, I was afraid about writing my second script, and it just took me a long time.

. . . I finally figured out late, if I would get stuck, the best thing I could do was to just call [the producers] and say, "Okay, I'm stuck," and they would start helping me unlock my mind.

And there were plenty of times where I thought, "I'm not going to be able to do this." I mean, I cried a river trying to figure out what I was going to do, how I was going to suffer the humiliation of everybody realizing that *Thelma and Louise* had just been a complete fluke and I actually didn't have any talent, and I was, you know . . . I mean, I went all the way to the bottom.

There were plenty of times when I thought, "Okay, I don't know what I'm going to do. I can't do this. I have gone all the way down this road, I have traveled halfway around the earth to find out that I'm going to hit a wall." It's a terrible feeling.

SBK: Was it like getting to seventy pages and you go . . . or thirty pages . . . or . . .

CK: No. It's after you've done one hundred sixty pages and you're not even into the third act yet. [Laughs.]

I was really, really scared. And really embarrassed that it was taking so long. It was just awful. But in spite of all that, I still consider myself an extremely fortunate, lucky person.

Because the fact is, even if I couldn't have finished this script, I'm still a fortunate person. I still see my many blessings. So the worst thing that happens is you don't finish a script. I think there are a lot of people in the world that are going through a lot worse than that. So I keep things in perspective, too.

SBK: You started out as an actress?

CK: I was in drama school in Purdue, and then I moved to Nashville for a few years and took acting class while I was there and did theatre. And then I moved out here and went to the Strasberg Institute and then studied with Peggy Feury . . . and then I quit. It just wasn't going to happen.

I was always confused about what it was I was doing. There weren't those parts that I was reading that I was just dying to do, so I thought there was something wrong with me. You know, that there was some part of it that I just wasn't understanding.

SBK: Because you weren't just loving it?

CK: Yes. I loved the act of giving of yourself that much, giving yourself over that much to something. But I wasn't getting to say the kind of things I wanted to say. It's not like I was reading parts that were making me go, "Oh my God, I would just kill to say that."

Well, what's available for young women? Not a fucking thing. Nothing that really talks about their experience of being in the world. I wasn't finding things that I was relating to. They certainly weren't what we were doing in acting class.

It's weird—I came to see women as fundamentally flawed through drama. All the women that were ever represented dramatically were so fucked up and pathetic and horrible and just messed up people that I just sort of thought, is that the way women really are?

Not to mention the fact that when you're doing plays and scenes, you'd be surprised at how often the opportunity to play a prostitute comes up. I'm like, "Oh, I get it. The only way women are really interesting is sexually, and it's not even when they're in control of it, it's when it's for sale." There are those who'd say "They are in control of it," in terms of it being for sale, but as far as I'm concerned, when your ass is for sale, you're a slave.

So after that, and working in music video, which is really the nadir of women's expression and the representation of women, I just don't think it can get a whole lot worse. And when you add on top of that the number of young girls who are willing to just exploit themselves for nothing other than the opportunity and feel like that's some form of accomplishment . . . I think *Thelma and Louise* was a really natural reaction to that, you know?

SBK: Yeah, I think there are a lot of stories about women that haven't been told. And about men, either.

CK: That's the thing that's really interesting to me, too, is that I am very interested in men as a subject. It's not like I'm interested only in women. It's just that there are so few people doing it that right now you might as well do it because at least you're doing something nobody else is doing. And something besides women as sex object kind of roles. You can always get movies made about prostitutes and strippers. That's not really much of a challenge.

SBK: And then there's this whole other subject, which is movies that are just not very nice to women, that set women up as the enemy.

CK: I know. That's why it's always really irritating for me to hear *Thelma and Louise* described as man-hating or anything I do described as man-hating, because it's like all the women-hating shit that's out there right now and you're going to bother me with that?

Some people might think we're hard on men in *Something to Talk About* . . . a guy gets kicked in the nuts, he gets poisoned . . . but I'm like, you know, a month before we started shooting this movie, a guy in Towson,

Maryland, shot his wife in the head with a hunting rifle, killed her, 'cause he caught her in bed with somebody else, and he got 18 months work release and the judge said he was sorry he had to sentence him at all. So kiss my ass.

SBK: What for you was the kernel of Something to Talk About?

CK: The family. I saw those characters right away. Except for Grace. Grace would not come for years. That was the other thing that really slowed me down. I started out thinking about women who have really willingly turned into that person. And I just couldn't feel any sympathy for her.

It was like, if she did that . . . and you can really hear me in Emma Rae, because I'm like, "Hey, man, you did this. You know, this is your fault." I kept saying, "Well, how am I supposed to care about her?"

It took me a long time to realize that I had to write a character that would be more like me in that it was parceled away. She gave it up incrementally, you know what I mean? She didn't just suddenly throw it all away and say, "I'm going to be this very conventional Charity League wife." But just a little tiny bit at a time, until one day she wakes up and she's like, "Accckkkkkk!"

. . . We talked about these women [for whom] that *is* their life. I mean, they honestly believe that sacrifice is the noble thing to do. And it is, for them. And saying, "This is the choice that you've made, and it's right, and even though it's painful, it's the right thing to do." There is a love that I have for those women, even though I would not want to be them, and I don't agree with it, I respect them. And I respect her.

We talked a lot about those women. You know, [for whom] public humiliation is the worst thing in the world. You can deal with anything if you deal with it in a dignified way. And it's just that fear of being exposed. . . .

SBK: When you say "we talked about it," did you talk about it with the actors, as well?

CK: Yeah. Lasse [Hallstrom], because he was from Sweden, because this was such a regional story, he was really open to me talking with all the actors about backstory and things like that. He wanted to hear as much as they did.

SBK: How different was your final draft from your first?

CK: Not that different. We added some scenes. This movie was a big studio picture, and we did test screenings. *Thelma and Louise* was such a flukey story, in a way. We were gonna have that ending if it had tested worse than anything in the world. But this was a big studio picture.

I think in my first draft, it ended the day after the party, after she said good-bye to him. I said, I really want the end of the movie to be that there is now a place to begin—that she's going to be going back to school and she and Eddie, if they decide they want to, they have a place now from which they can start that they did not have at the beginning of this movie. The playing field is now level.

And what we did, based on the responses, we just went ahead and showed it.

That's a real love story to me, you know what I mean? Where it doesn't require one person to be not fully functioning to make the relationship work.

SBK: So what about writing is, for you, the really hardest part?

CK: Making myself actually do it now. Making myself sit down and actually write. There's a big element of fear involved for me with it, you know. I'm very afraid that it's not going to be there. Or that, the same thing that every writer in the world goes through, not just because the first one was so incredibly well received, but that it was noticed at all. I felt very self-conscious, and I still feel self-conscious.

And I don't know what I'm going to write next. I'm not a person that's got ideas stacked up on top of ideas, just waiting to get a chance to write them. You know, it's like I really enter into a relationship with a story. It's like I'm in a marriage with that story; I've got to be really sure about it. I still take it a little too seriously, I guess.

SBK: What are you proudest of, of all you've done?

CK: That I've completed screenplays. That I've finished them at all. That's the thing that I just can't get over. 'Cause the joy of actually finishing something is mind-boggling to me, and I feel like a little kid, who just . . . . My drawing is hanging on the refrigerator, thank you very much, ladies and gentlemen.

A CONVERSATION WITH . . .

Mike Leigh

Make no mistake: Mike Leigh is not easy. But then, neither are his movies. They're a complex ganglion of characters, not all of them likable. Somehow, however, they are care-inducing.

And the movies have reaped big awards for the British filmmaker: a National Society of Film Critics' Best Film ('91) for *Life Is Sweet,* a Best Director Award at Cannes ('93) for *Naked,* and, this year, Cannes' Palme d'Or for *Secrets & Lies.*

Even if you haven't yet seen one of his films, you probably have heard of parts of them. It's in his *Life Is Sweet,* for example, that Jane Horrocks appears covered in chocolate. But, as he is quick to note, you don't have to be a chocolate lover to create a scene like that. Nor, by implication, a misogynist to create the character of Johnny (played by David Thewlis) in *Naked.*

A student at the Royal Academy of Dramatic Art in the '60s, Mike Leigh started out creating plays in much the same way that he still creates his movies. In the '70s and '80s, much of his work also appeared to high acclaim on British television. With *Secrets & Lies* getting ready to open in the U.S., he sat in the Hotel Nikko fresh from Telluride, talked about his process of making movies, and brooked no imprecision.

SBK: Here's my experience of watching one of your films, whether it's Life Is Sweet, High Hopes, Naked, _or_ Secrets & Lies: _I start out watching the movie thinking "Who are these characters, and what am I doing watching such weird people on the screen?" And then about halfway through, something clicks in, and I'm right there—in their living room, at their dining room table, at the birthday party in_ High Hopes, _or the coffeeshop in_ Secrets & Lies—_caring mightily about these people. So how do you do that? How do you make us care about these people?_

MIKE LEIGH: Well, I suppose the only thing I can say about that is I can only make you care by caring about them myself. And by believing in them. I mean, we work so thoroughly with them that we arrive at a condition where we really do believe in these people. We invent them—they're a figment of our imagination—but we do actually, completely, get to believe in them and they have thorough, organic lives. The emotions, the charge, the electricity of the tensions . . . and also the love and the distrust and all the other things are actually happening, because they really are in there.

Unless you care about something yourself, there's really no reason why the audience should be expected to. And, indeed, you are only disposed to notice it or discuss it as if it were extraordinary because so many films don't do that for you, and the reason why so many films don't do it for you is because they don't really believe in it themselves. That's my only answer.

SBK: I'm interested in the process through which you write and direct your movies. I've read a fair number of pieces about you and I understand that you start with . . . let me ask you, where do you start?

ML: What were you going to say? It might be easier for me to respond to what you thought.

SBK: I understand that you start basically with your notion and then you call in the actors that you want to use and talk with them one-on-one. True?

ML: Yes, but that's not really the essence of it. What we do is to work for a certain period of time before the shoot to create . . . the one-on-one is only a technicality. The point is that they work together in character, and we explore these worlds and bring them into existence.

For me, the writing process and the directing process are the same thing. As far as I'm concerned, the script is the film. The film is the script. There isn't a script that you then make a film from the script. The script *is* the film.

I cannot finally write the scenes unless I'm actually working on them and can see them visually in that location. In other words, the writing has to say what they say. And the visual, physical, the action are inextricably one and the same. So there is never a script in the conventional sense. I mean, there is a published script, but that's something I've sat down and written up after the event.

But what we shoot is completely precise. The literary qualities, the literary considerations, the writing qualities are very, very important, and I deal with those in as writerly a way as I can. But always on the floor, working with them, and writing through directing.

SBK: What are some of those considerations?

ML: Well, I'm talking about the quality of words and the opposition of ideas and the rhythm . . . the enjoyment of the language. There is a poetic side to what we do. But it has to be in character. You look at Johnny [in *Naked*]—he breaks out of that flat and goes down and hangs around the street corner and runs into Archie and then Maggie—there's a lot of language stuff going on which is kind of heightened and works at a number of levels—but it comes out of an organic, three-dimensional creating of this through the actors acting in character.

We rehearsed *Secrets & Lies* for five months before we started shooting. A lot of that time is living through the lives of the characters and building up this whole history, this backstory.

And my job is to direct the actors, often one-on-one, in how to play the character, how to do the characterization, working with them on behavior as well as everything else. And built into that are implicit writing decisions. But just as a writer, an ordinary writer, a conventional writer, will sit down and . . . I mean, what I do is what everybody does, really. Which is to say, to write a script, you sit down, you start improvising, and you discover what it is by writing it.

And that's all I do, really! The only difference is the actors are involved. And, indeed, the other people are involved, too. But basically we're doing exactly the very same thing. It's just that I don't do it in isolation and then have the problem of finding the actors. It all meshes together.

SBK: When you were first starting out with Secrets & Lies, *what was the very first step?*

ML: Well, the first actual manifest thing is, indeed, working one-on-one with some of the actors. In that case, [Timothy] Spall and [Brenda] Blethyn, 'cause logically they come first in the chronology. . . . And what I actually do specifically, I'm not disposed to talk about. But in principle, I set about working with the actors to invent, create, and bring to life each character and put them together and build up their mutual world and explore it through discussion and through a lot of research, but mostly through a huge amount of improvisation.

SBK: So when you were working with Brenda Blethyn and you went to her originally, how much of the story had you formulated in your head?

ML: What it sounds as though you're really asking, though you didn't say that, is how much did I tell her? And the bottom line is: nothing. The deal is, for me with actors, is to say, "Look, come and be in the film. I can't tell you what it's about, I can't tell you what your part's going to be, I can't tell you anything, these are the dates, and if you're on for it, some-one will talk with your agent about the money." That is the deal, that's always the deal. And if an actor doesn't feel comfortable with that, then basically they can go on to other sorts of films where they know what they're doing, because there are loads of actors who do want to do it and are very good at it. But, of course, that isn't to say that there aren't things kicking around in my head. But I never say anything about that to any-body, including my producer or indeed the backers, because that leaves me free to expand and contract and explore possibilities. Obviously I'm motivated by certain things, but nobody ever knows what they are. So it has the advantage of being a journey into the unknown.

So we make the film, we discover what the film is, by making it.

Obviously there are actors with whom I click, and actors with whom I don't click. And I try, best as I can, to get hold of the wavelength ones. That's what it's about. It's horses for courses, as we say.

It takes a lot of meetings to get a character on the go, a lot of sessions. I did have a first meeting with the entire cast, at which no discussion takes place about the film itself, merely about the mechanics—how we're going to go about it.

And another thing that's terribly important in making all this work is that it is essential throughout the entire process that none of the actors ever knows anything about anything except what his or her character would know about.

SBK: So they really do make that unknown journey.

<u>ML:</u> Yes. So that it's spontaneous. So that when you get in *Secrets & Lies* the sequence where they all come 'round to the barbecue, where Cynthia introduces Hortense . . . having shot three-quarters of the movie . . . when we set up rehearsal days within the shoot in the location, they all came 'round in character to do an improvisation out of which I could construct and build a scene . . . and at the time of that initial improvisation, none of them knew who Hortense was.

We had maintained that secrecy for a considerable length of time, including having shot three-quarters of the picture. Which involved a security system that the CIA and FBI would together be defeated by, really.

And of course it works. Because it means that they've got this real experience to draw from.

SBK: So, from what you're saying, three-quarters of the way through you take the time necessary to improvise it and create that scene?

<u>ML:</u> Yes.

SBK: So you don't just shoot a movie straight through at all.

<u>ML:</u> No.

SBK: Well, it sounds like an ideal way for a writer to work.

<u>ML:</u> Yes. I mean, the point is this: there are labels for things. There's a label called *writer,* there's a label called *director,* there's a label called *storyteller,* and there's a label called *filmmaker.* I am a writer in that I'm a storyteller.

I'm a writer in that I'm concerned with language and character. I am a director in that I do all the things a director . . . but I don't actually divide up these things. You say this is ideal for a writer—I kind of think that's sort of all right, but probably I'm uncomfortable with the statement, because it's good for a *filmmaker,* who happens also within that to write.

But it wouldn't work for a lot of writers, because a lot of writers are pretty ivory tower and prefer the solitary nature of it, which I don't. And a lot of writers don't get on with actors or can't direct or aren't visual and all those things, and therefore it wouldn't work for those writers. Though I have perfectly adequate writing skills and writing sensibilities, I'm not as good if I sit in a room with a pen or a typewriter, and I'm computer illiterate because I don't need to be otherwise. I do better writing working the way I do.

But that's because it happens to suit my particular interests and needs. So I'm slightly cautious when you say that's the ideal situation for a writer. It isn't. It's the ideal situation for my particular sort of storyteller.

SBK: To be more accurate, it sounds like the ideal situation for this *writer, because I love working with actors, also, in theatre here and creating together.*

ML: Now, in the specific context of those of us that are built this way, as it were, it's absolute common sense. Let's be clear about this before we go any further. I mean, we aren't inventing the wheel. That is for sure how they would have been doing it thousands of years ago and in the medieval theatre. And there's no question that such things went on at the Globe, and no doubt whatever that Chaplin and Keaton and all kinds of other folk set about creating movies in an organic, "let's see what happens, let's make it up as we go along" kind of way until the talkies came along and everybody started getting twitchy about the page and the word. So it's not news, really.

SBK: Getting back to the barbeque scene and the revelation . . . after you bring them together, and they improvise their surprise . . .

ML: They improvise the whole thing. If you were a fly on the wall, which I am, you are seeing actors so good and thorough in their characters that it is a real event taking place. And of course what happens in that improvisation is just the improvisation. It's never the same as what you get in the film. My job is to then take that and challenge it and use it and expand it, contract it, refine it, so what you get isn't *it* but some quite other thing of which that was source material. And you do several main improvisations from which to work. It's a terribly complicated process and I really can't summarize it too easily. But it takes time.

In that example, that whole thing was that barbeque culture, so they had to be outdoors. But I felt, dramatically, that the revelation itself, when the shit hits the fan, would not be better served outdoors, it needed to be interior. So I had to invent that the phone starts ringing. And also it gave me the opportunity to vary the rhythm . . . at the barbeque, wide shot, construct it as it all happens within that shot . . . but when we go inside, we can have a montage there . . . so all of that. Of course, in an improvisation that lasted eight hours, all kinds of stuff happens—apart from anything else, it's deeply repetitious and boring and wrong. But the job is to use that as an inspiration and a source of material from which in turn to distill and construct.

You actually do lots of improvisations to re-investigate different aspects of it. And you can change what happens—if I change the motivation, the timing, or whatever it is. . . .

SBK: And is it conceivable that you would say, "No, wait a minute—what if this happens and this? . . ."

ML: All the time! That's what it's about. Otherwise, it wouldn't have the coherence . . . it wouldn't be well written and directed by. So I do that all the time. And if I say, "Well, could this happen?" And they say, "No." And I say, "Why not?" And they say, "Because he wouldn't do that." So I say, "Well, fair enough,"—I always accept that—"however, to change the conditions, if she had said so-and-so," or "if this happened earlier," . . . "Oh, yeah—then it would be right."

So therefore what it's about is being absolutely *au fait* with, in tune with, the characters.

SBK: Do you actually then give them lines to say?

ML: Well, if you do what we're talking about and build up and rehearse and rehearse, a lot of the dialogue is distilled from the improvisation. And then I might say, "Well, instead of saying that, why don't you say this?"

Or actually what it sometimes comes down to is "We just need to put another line in." I always say, "Just try it—see what happens." I have to constantly keep an eye on the rhythm and style.

Half the time I'm just going, "Okay, that's fine, but you can't say that 'cause that's a repetition of what you said earlier." Ordinary writing stuff.

SBK: So that means that in the coffeeshop sequence where Cynthia learns that Hortense is her daughter, she didn't know . . . Brenda Blethyn didn't know?

ML: When we did the original improvisation of that, yes. It was a bit more complex than that because of course we had already decided that she had had this experience, but we decided that she will have forgotten it. So technically, in that particular instance, the actress can't forget what she knew—but she was able to sustain it as though she didn't.

SBK: It was, by the way, wonderful watching her on the screen come to this realization.

ML: Well, of course, all of this kind of bullshit that I'm describing to you to get there pales into insignificance beside what really matters, which is what does or doesn't happen on the screen, when the camera turns. That's what matters.

SBK: You wrote your first screenplay in your twenties. . . .

ML: Well, if you don't mind my saying so, given the conversation that we're having, I made my first film in my twenties, I did not write my first screenplay. I've never written a screenplay. I made *Bleak Moments* when I was twenty-eight.

SBK: And was it similar, the process you went through for Bleak Moments?

ML: Oh, yeah. I've been doing it since 1965, this way of working.

SBK: Has your process changed since then?

ML: Not in principle. It obviously has in the sense that whatever you do gets better by refinement. But no, in principle it's exactly the same.

SBK: What kinds of things have gotten easier and/or better?

ML: Well, you get more time. And of course I get a huge choice of actors. And I've developed skills and opened things up a bit more in different ways. But in some ways it gets harder. Because in order to do what we're talking about, it is incredibly hard work, and there's a great deal of work, as we've identified earlier in the conversation, that is one-to-one with actors. Or you just work with certain pockets of the action for a while.

And because it's bad practice to be kept hanging around. . . . For example, Marianne Jean-Baptiste winds up with a big slice of the cake in the film, but for quite a lot of the time when it was in rehearsal, she was hanging around for weeks, not doing anything, because I was dealing with the family. So therefore, it means I have to try as much as I can to work morning, noon, and night, because it reduces the amount of waiting time. And I do work at least six days a week, and this goes on for months. I invented this way of working when I was in my early twenties, and now I'm fifty-three, and frankly it does get very, very hard.

And that's only the preparation. Then there's the shooting, where, as you've identified, we rehearse during the shoot. Well, that is quite a heavy thing to do because shooting is valuable, so you rehearse at nights, you rehearse on weekends—and that means you don't get a day off from it the entire shoot. So it is knackering, basically; it's very tiring.

On the other hand, when we made *Bleak Moments* we made it with a skeleton crew. . . . Now we have the most wonderful crews that are really committed. Also the catering is better.

SBK: Do you get noodgy when you're not making a movie?

ML: No, not now. What used to get me twitchy is the worry that I would not be making a movie, but that's not a problem. No, I like the other time. I mean, it does include doing this, which is a mixed blessing.

SBK: So then you make your movie and it goes to Cannes and wins a Palme d'Or. What does that do for you?

ML: Well, it's fine, it's wonderful. Good news—it means that people are going to see it, know about it, and that's what we make films for. So it's wonderful. It's very gratifying. And the dinners are good in Cannes.

SBK: What is the most gratifying part of making a movie for you?

<u>ML:</u> Well, that's a hard one. What isn't gratifying? What is a chore is that preparation. What is a joy is shooting. The esprit de corps—the whole thing. I just love it. And being in the cutting room is always a joy because you've got material, so it's like being on holiday.

But in the end, one of the great joys of making a film, certainly for me, is to sit in an audience and get the feedback. Or in the case, say, of this film—to hear from people who call and say, "You know, I've decided to seek out my birth mother." Or people saying, "I laughed and cried simultaneously." Well, that, to me, that is the joy of making a film, you know, because that's what it's about.

A CONVERSATION WITH . . .

Anthony Minghella

Just in case you might think that a man who ponders such things as the importance of fiction, and who taught theatre history and dramatic literature at the university level, and who wrote the pilot episode of *Inspector Morse* might be, well, academic, ponder this: one of Anthony Minghella's memories from growing up on England's Isle of Wight was as a teenager, selling ice cream for his dad at the Isle of Wight Festival of Music in the years surrounding Woodstock. And he stands there, handing out ice cream cones to a family he realizes is entirely naked. "There's nothing quite so absurd," he says, "as a naked family eating ice cream cones, and I've never forgotten that, that image." And then he laughs, thinking of it, "Those days are gone. They won't come again, I don't think."

Neither, probably, will the day, during the same Festival, when the fourteen-year-old rock musician went down to the beach with his buddy at 4 A.M. to wait for Bob Dylan, who, they'd heard, was arriving by Hovercraft. Big times for the Isle of Wight, and big times for Anthony Minghella, who's gone on to a clutch of big times himself.

Two days after *The English Patient* had won a Golden Globe for best drama, and minutes after he'd been nominated for a Directors Guild of America (DGA) award, and two weeks before being nominated for a

WGA best adaptation award, Anthony Minghella talked about adapting a book previously thought of as unadaptable, the responsibility of fiction, and the truth behind the statement in his foreword to the published screenplay of *The English Patient.*

SBK: Is it really true that when you went to write the screenplay, you left the book [by Michael Ondaatje] behind?

ANTHONY MINGHELLA: It's true. It's a distillation of a series of trips that I wrote about in the introduction to the published screenplay. The common and conventional wisdom about this book was that it was not possible to adapt it, that it defied adaptation. I was an admirer of Michael's writing—I had read everything he'd written before *The English Patient,* and I read it for fun and not as a job. I had plunged into it long before I thought how I might do it as a film. But having plunged into the well of it, I really felt strongly there was a film there, and I could see a film, but what I was alert to was the fact that the book is largely connected with the poetry and beauty of words, and film on the whole is not as adroit at working in verbal terms as it is in communicating itself with image. And I think the job of the screenwriter is much more architectural than it is the work of poetry.

Cinema is capable of poetry. If you can hand over to the director a map which has all of the territory properly corralled and choreographed, then the filmmaker can use that blueprint to create something which has its own poetry. Often that's the poetry of transition, of one image sitting against another, and what each says to the other. So what I tried to do was to find a way of translating Michael's book not in a literal sense but in a way when I'd made the film it would have some of the lyricism that the book had had.

The other thing that distinguishes novels is their ability to conjure worlds with a minimum of writing. Michael is particularly clever and gifted at doing this. In a single line he can evoke a place, he can evoke a personality—in a metonymic way, in a sense—where a crown suggests the king, or a castle suggests the kingdom. And what you do when you read is that you exercise your imagination by creating the world that the novelist is hinting at.

The quality of film is much more literal, I think. You only see what's in front of the camera. Obviously the obligation of the filmmaker is twofold: one is to find a story, because storytelling is much more significant in film than it is in the contemporary novel. And the other thing is that you have to create worlds. I remember *Time* magazine talked about *The English Patient*, the novel, as being a magic carpet ride in an imaginative sense. I think in a film the magic carpet ride is literal—you have to take people to other worlds.

So what I did was I tried to educate myself about the territories and circumstances of the film, not only in terms of geography but also in terms of history, so I had to travel a lot and I had to read a lot. And when it came to doing the first draft of the adaptation, having been to some of the locations mentioned in the book, I then tried to arm myself with as much reference material and source material as I could. I read lots of diaries and journals and literature about the Second World War. I read a great deal about Cairo before the War, and I went to the Royal Geographic Society and read about documents of exploration. I read some of the reports of explorers who were beginning to circumnavigate the Sahara.

And all the time I was relishing Michael's book and learning it, in a way. But when it came to sitting down to write the screenplay, I felt that if I had the book with me, I would've been so enthralled to it, and so prone to copying out large chunks of beautiful writing. So what I tried to do was, armed with all this research material, write my way back to the book. And I felt in the process what would happen is that the events and moments in the book which had arrested me would find their way in a new form in the screenplay.

I'll give you an example. There is a wonderful episode in the book which has nothing to do with the central characters, which is about Kip in Italy, long before he arrives in Hana's life, working at defusing bombs in a church. Art historians are there to patrol the care of the precious objects in the church and the paintings in the church, and he hoists one of the art historians up so that he can examine a fresco at close quarters.

Well, that's not a scene that a film like this can accommodate, but the idea of hoisting, and the idea of Kip making a gift to somebody, was a perfect way, I felt, in the film, of illustrating a particular kind of love which somebody has for somebody else. And it becomes, I think, in the film a lovemaking scene without physical contact.

And given that it's a film which rehearses all manner of love, rehearses all types of loving exchange, and because the central loving exchange in the film is carnal and erotic and catastrophic and tumultuous and larva-like, I was trying to find some corollary in the relationship between Kip and Hana which is much more tender and innocent, and this sense of transporting that's in that scene comes as a balance to the other relationship between Almasy and Katharine.

SBK: And it works. I have a question, though. In the book, I thought as I was reading it that Almasy was a spy, but he's not in the movie. How did you decide to make that change?

AM: Well, the writing of the screenplay and the directing of the film has been a process of distillation, a process of refinement over a period of years. So the screenplay itself changed many, many times, and the emphases in the screenplay changed. We talked about the obligation to create a world. The other obligation is to tell a story, and to be able to pursue a story transparently with a complex structure, because obviously the film is a very ambitious one in the way that it tells the story. It isn't a "and then and then and then" beginning, middle, and end story; it's a puzzle. And solving the puzzle and making sense of the puzzle is one of the pleasures, I hope, for the filmgoer.

But there's only so much that you can convey to an audience in the period of time allocated to you, unlike the pleasure of reading a novel where you can meditate in tranquillity. It's stated by implication in the book, and in the film implication is much more difficult to deal with. I tried to find a single action which had characterized what had happened, and the single action was the handing over of maps to the Germans. Because it seemed to me that that was the central transgression of Almasy—he made maps with friends of all nationalities, and he gave those maps to a particular side in the war. So the betrayal is most sharp and acute at that moment. And, given the point in the film, two-thirds of the way or three-fourths of the way into the film, that action stands in for a whole host of other actions. He's there as a cartographer, he has great antipathy for the idea of maps belonging to nations. . . . And having had that ideological manifesto, he then does quite the reverse and hands his maps over, and in doing so betrays his closest friend. That seemed to me to be a very clear index of the cost of his own loyalty and the cost of his own betrayal. That's all. I think that you need clear flags in a story like this, and that seemed to me to be the clearest one I could think of.

<u>SBK</u>: *And besides, what woman wouldn't want to think that a man would do such a huge, huge turnabout in the name of love?*

<u>AM</u>: Well, I think the film asks questions. It says: is it better to betray your country than to betray your friend? And one of the things that I feel very strongly about, as somebody who works in fiction, is that fiction has a responsibility. It's not a responsibility to biography, it's not a responsibility to history—it's a responsibility to audiences and to its place in culture, because I think the question which is very rarely asked is: what is fiction for? We all assume that it has some place and some purpose—we don't question it, we just get on with making it. But if you tell stories for a living, I think you are duty bound to consider what the purpose of fiction is. And I think that if fiction is closed, and by that I mean if it makes its moral judgments and adjudications within itself, then the audience is necessarily passive—it's not required to think about what he or she as an audience member is watching—it's only listening to a point of view which is fully articulated. And that doesn't seem to be a useful function.

I think that if fiction asks you to make judgments, if it asks you to reconsider an event from more than one viewpoint, if it asks you to imagine the overwhelming inexorable momentum towards embracing somebody that morally you might feel resistant to, if your instinct is confronted by your responsibility, if you see people struggling with the pain of dealing with instinct and responsibility in crisis, and at the same time having inhabited that viewpoint, you're forced to then reconsider exactly the same action from the point of view of the person who's being betrayed—from a husband sitting in a cab while he knows that his wife is with somebody else—then what it does for you is rather than pass judgment on the woman in this sequence or passing judgment on the man, it says, "Look at the difficulty of behaving well." "Look at the fact that often in pursuing our own volitions, we trample on the volitions of somebody else." "Look at the capacity people have to hurt each other and to heal each other."

And notice that all these things can be done with a certain amount of integrity, and in fact, in the film, with a great deal of integrity. Katharine is so allied to candor and to the truth that she, in the sweetest moment that she shares with Almasy, when he's asking her to tell him all the things that she loves, the first idea in her mind is the fact that she loves her husband. Because that's never far below the surface of any exchange she has with Almasy. The fact that she'll say that to him, the fact that she won't lie, the fact that ultimately she gives him up because she would rather bear her own pain than inflict pain on her husband means that this is a morally complex woman.

And I think that the difficulty in Hollywood filmmaking, and it's not a criticism of Hollywood filmmaking, is that it's made an association between success and moral clarity. It thinks that the way forward is to suggest that the world is divided into people who behave well and people who behave badly, and so you get very good people and very bad people.

Well, I've almost never met somebody who's either very good or very bad. And my concern is to identify the turmoil of the moral position, the turmoil of trying to live well, and offer it up for analysis from more than one perspective. So that people perhaps become more human and more generous in the way that they look at other people. Because I think that the responsibility of fiction . . . the only reason why we want to sit down in the dark and look at other people's lives is because we need some enlargement of our own—we need to expand the frame of reference by which we can look at our own lives. And if the place we go to for that expansion is not telling the truth, is not being evenhanded in the way that it tells its stories, then we are getting false currency.

And so my only thought as a writer is to try to accurately tell stories, accurately show behavior, accurately show the vicissitudes of thought and emotion.

SBK: When you were working on this script, who did you trust to give you feedback on it?

AM: Michael Ondaatje I trusted completely. I began this project because I felt passionate about the book. So if I had ended up with a successful film that he didn't like, I would have felt that that was a failure. And the fact that the book is doing so marvelously well is the thing that I'm most proud of. At the same time, I was very clear with him at the beginning that I was going to have to write this screenplay by myself, and that in the process would be unraveling a great deal of what's beautiful about his book. No film could accommodate or lasso all of the material that's in the book.

Also, I've had to invent material to fill out some of what are only inferred parts in the book. So not only was I ditching, right, left, and center, wonderful material from the novel, I was also bringing new scenes into the screenplay. Saul Zaentz encouraged me to do this, to involve

Michael, so that he was part of the navigation of that, rather than being a writer whose book was wrested away from him and then returned, bleeding.

SBK: You said also that Saul Zaentz encouraged you to be fearless.

AM: Absolutely.

SBK: In what way?

AM: Fearless in the sense of not second-guessing somebody's response to what I was doing. You know, you can get very preoccupied with the other end of a film, with the end result. You can get very preoccupied with what happens when somebody sits down in front of what you've done. His encouragement to me was an empowering one, which was that you're doing this project because you have a vision of it. Be rigorous about the vision, don't be rigorous about the result.

I hope that that would be my policy without Saul. It's just that the invasion of producers' judgment, the invasion of a distributor's judgment, is something that I think all filmmakers dread. With Saul, he doesn't invade, he collaborates and supports. And that's a unique quality.

SBK: How did you hook up with him in the first place?

AM: He hooked up with me, which was a thrilling thing. He had seen *Truly, Madly, Deeply* several times and he called me in London and said he was coming and could we get together, and so we talked about doing things together about a year before I found the novel *The English Patient.* And we have a great deal in common, because I'm somebody who's very interested in music, and he owns, with partners, Fantasy Records. He's been involved with jazz all his life. So we discovered all sorts of mutual passions when we met, and he was the first person I thought of when I read the book.

SBK: You started out teaching theatre history?

AM: Yes, and dramatic literature. And then I wrote plays. From my early 20's I was writing plays, working in the theatre. And some of that work started to be done on TV, then I was writing TV shows, then I met Jim

[Henson]. I was still very much involved as a playwright then—in fact, in the year that I began working with Jim Henson, I had a play on in the West End and a series of plays on Channel 4. The play in the West End was about the exploitation of women in Thailand. . . .

SBK: Made in Bangkok.

AM: Yes. The plays on Channel 4 were a series of plays about divorce and reconciliation, and Jim asked me if I wanted to write a children's series about fairy tales. I thought it was a very bizarre notion, but it was one that I was extremely grateful for, because I managed to spend some time with him and become very close to him. I'm still involved with the Hensons now. My office is there in London. And Duncan Kenworthy, who produced *The Storyteller* and went on to produce *Four Weddings and a Funeral,* has his office there, as well. So there's a community of filmmakers and writers who work in the Henson building in London, and it's a very important oasis, I think.

SBK: At what point did you decide you were ready to direct?

AM: I directed before I wrote. When I was a student, I was directing. I had no thoughts of becoming a writer. My thoughts were about how to make music, how to direct music, how to be involved as a musician and a director in the theatre and film, or something. I had written a series of songs that I wanted to lace together into some event to direct, and in the lacing together, I found myself writing scenes. And what happened was I found something in that process which really intrigued me, and almost accidentally found myself writing for a living. And the thing that I would say without any hesitation is I'm a writer who directs. I think it would be tragic for me if I didn't direct another film; I think it would be impossible for me to stop writing.

I certainly don't have facility as a writer. I'm not a writer from whom ink pours. I have to work very hard as a writer. But it's the only time I feel myself. I have more fun as a director because it's collaborative and you're working in a public arena and you can laugh more and there's a sense of people shouldering the burden with you. When you're a writer you're necessarily alone, and so I don't relish those periods of aloneness, but it's also when I feel most close to myself, most close to doing what I was designed to do.

SBK: When you're writing, what is your writing day like?

AM: Well, I've never had a proper job in my life, and so I would say that I'm a lazy person who works all the time. I can't remember the last day I had a day off. You understand this? I can't remember the last day I didn't think about the next piece of work that I was involved in. But I'm incapable of working to a routine. And I've long since forgiven myself for that. I was raised as a Catholic, and I'm plagued, as all Catholics are, by the most labyrinthine guilt. I'm tormented by my inadequacies as a person, but tormenting myself as a writer has been a futile activity. So what I do is allow myself to work in the way it comes to me, and every job has been different.

What I'm trying to say in an extremely circuitous and awkward way is that often I'll be in the process of approaching work and leaving work for hours and hours and hours and hours. And I have this rosary of diversionary tactics—I'll do anything rather than sit down and think. And I think that in a sense what I'm alert to is that I have this very clear sense that everything is already written, that it exists, this screenplay of *The English Patient,* and it's in a drawer in my room, and the only problem is I'm only allowed to look at it for two or three seconds every day. And in order for the drawer to open, you have to sit and wait for it.

So there's a lot of time spent roaming, waiting for the drawer to slide open, then you see some lines and you write them down as quickly as you can, and the drawer slams. And sometimes the drawer opens and it stays open for hours, and then it doesn't matter what time of the day or night it is, you just wait and thank God that it's there and you can write some of the stuff down. And other days will go by where the drawer never opens. And that's the only analogy I can think of, the only metaphor for what I think the writing process is: it requires all your attention all the time for very little reward. And occasionally you go into a spell of blessing, and you have to stay with it then, and there are times when I would write for two or three days without doing anything other than brushing my teeth.

SBK: No sleep?

AM: Any writer who's ever read this magazine will know that sleep, when you're working, is a very low priority.

A CONVERSATION WITH . . .

Ron Bass

Ron Bass knows his numbers. Knows that six of his script pages, handwritten, equal four script pages, typed. And knows that if you get up at 3:45 in the morning, you can get a fair bit done by 9:45.

He didn't used to get up at 3:45. But then, he didn't used to be a screenwriter, either. Used to be an entertainment lawyer. An entertainment lawyer who'd once written a novel at age seventeen, then burned it and didn't write again for sixteen years. And even then, wrote mainly on weekends and odd hours.

It was only when he began writing his third novel that he began to realize what a difference a dawn makes, and changed his routine to incorporate it daily. Now it's so ingrained he calls his company Predawn Productions, which in the last couple years has grown to six employees and has six movies in various stages of development. Just how this all works in the interest of writing movies is something I asked him about in his backyard garden one spring morning, after he'd just gotten in from New York the day before, where he'd had meetings on *Stepmom*, a rewrite of a movie for TriStar.

SBK: So it's 9:45. What have you already done today?

RON BASS: Well, I've been at work since 3:45. So I've been at work for six hours. [Laughs.]

SBK: What time did you go to sleep in order to get up at 3:45?

RB: Last night I got to sleep at midnight and it was really bad because I had just come in from New York. So I was really tired!

I got up this morning and reviewed more notes on *Stepmom* and did some of the work toward that rewrite. There's also a script called *First Lady*, a first draft that I just finished about the first woman president. My partner Leonard Goldberg, the other producer, had some questions about certain things.

I also am working today by telephone and fax with my partner Terry McMillan on the film that's going to start at the end of June, *How Stella Got Her Groove Back*. So she and I were redoing some scenes.

And I was on the phone this morning with my producing partner on *What Dreams May Come*, that's starting in June. Suddenly somebody at Interscope got the idea, "Should we do a certain scene differently?" And it's a very important issue, actually . . . and it may not sound like writing, but it is writing. So that got worked on this morning.

SBK: When I'm working on a script, I need what some people call "flow"— focus and concentration. How do you find your focus? Do you need a certain amount of time to focus on the Stepmom *rewrite, for instance, where nobody can bother you, or how do you do that?*

RB: There isn't any really one answer to that. For example, when we were in New York, Jane [Rusconi] and I and Chris Columbus literally were focusing on the *Stepmom* draft for thirteen hours without stopping. The longest stopping was a two-minute ride from my hotel to Julia Roberts' office, and we were talking all through that, anyway. Whenever anybody was eating, we were talking while we were eating. So there is a thirteen-hour uninterrupted collaborative focus.

I have been involved in alone writing—eighteen hours in a stretch— that's happened to me many times without ever breaking for anything. On the other hand, sometimes you're returning sixty phone calls and you're jumping into a very precise focus for five minutes on something that you've got to be very there and very centered on exactly what that emotional or structural or character or dramatic issue is, and you punch the other button and it's your producer on the other project and you're right into that.

One of the things that's helped me get to that place, and maybe part of the reason why I enjoy working on so many things at once, is that for seventeen years I was an entertainment lawyer. People who have never done entertainment law don't really know how different that is from a John Grisham trial lawyer. I was never in a courtroom. For seventeen years, I negotiated deals. And what that looks like is you have fifty files neatly on your desk in the morning. You have four or five phone lights that are always flashing, and all day long, you are punching a number and you are into the middle of some negotiation so deep and so argumentatively, and when that's done, you punch another one.

I did that for seventeen years, so it is completely natural for me to snap focus and just be completely living in one particular discussion.

For writing, it's even easier because the way that I write, it has an auto-writing component. There's a component of just being there and watching it happen. It is sort of like it's happening to you, and you are all the characters. You are feeling what they feel. You're saying the words in your mind with the accompanying emotions. And while you're doing it, while you're kind of role-playing all the roles, unconsciously and very rapidly in your mind, you are simultaneously like the director or the God kind of person who's somewhere watching it. You're watching it and you're being it at the same time and you're conscious of neither. But it isn't the intellectual process that you have doing law work, where you're actually rationally thinking through something.

It's a very natural feeling and it's very easy to be totally lost in it, particularly if you are alone. That's why I like to write in the garden that you see me in or in parks . . . but I could be on the deck of a ship, I could be in the back seat of a car, as long as I kind of shut myself into a world of my own.

SBK: And what do you write on?

RB: Physically? I do not know how to work a computer. Each of my scripts has its own loose-leaf binder, like a schoolboy, so I write on yellow loose-leaf paper with pencils. Each notebook has its two little plastic pencil cases in it, one for sharp pencils and one for dull pencils, and that's how I write.

SBK: And you know your page count?

RB: Yes, I actually count lines and I'm able to know how many pages of that translates into a typed page, after a lot of years doing it.

SBK: I read something with Terry McMillan where she said, "Oh, Ron told me that scene had to be 1.3 pages". . . .

RB: Oh, yes. When I originally outline something, I always page-budget it before I start writing, so I have a three-act outline with what all the scenes are going to be, and then I estimate how many pages to the half-page that I want each scene to be. Now, of course, that estimate doesn't hold, and some scenes will get shorter and some will get longer. Hardly anything is exactly what you guessed it was going to be.

But making that guess does a couple of valuable things. The obvious thing is it lets you know in a gross way whether you have too much or too little story. If you page-budget and you've got 160 pages, well, you know that you have to rethink the story, because it's longer than a movie's going to be. Or if you have 85 pages (that's never happened to me!), you'd know you had too little story.

But the thing that's more relevant is it's the beginning step that forces you to start thinking through the story in a chronological and coherent way to decide whether the first scene is 4 pages or 2 pages. And you have to start to deal with what's really gonna go in this. And that very process is the first step of really understanding it.

Then after that—I used to do this alone, but now I have this team that does it with me—I block the scene, by which I mean I really do prewrite. I figure it out before I ever start to write the script: What are all the things that are going to go into this scene? What's everybody gonna feel? Where's the start? Where does it end? What's the informational content? The emotional content? The dramatic tone? What are the character changes? What's everybody thinking and feeling? What's the setting gonna look like?

Now I talk about that in a staff meeting. And while I'm writing one or two scripts earlier, they are each sending me a fax on every single scene that we've outlined. And their fax will contain everything I've ever said, all the research they were assigned to do, and any ideas of their own they want me to consider, which could be very different from anything we've ever said before.

SBK: For each scene?

RB: For every single scene of this movie.

SBK: Can you give me an example?

RB: The best example is the movie that's coming out right now called *My Best Friend's Wedding,* which was a spec script I did with the team. The first scene of the movie, Julia Roberts is sitting with Rupert Everett, who plays her editor, in a restaurant. She's a food critic, and it's the interweaving of the information that we want to reveal about her past relationship with the character that Dermot Mulroney plays, who she had an affair with nine years ago when they were in college.

The affair ended, but they decided to remain best friends. They had this crazy drunken night six years ago where he made her promise that when they were twenty-eight years old, if neither of them had ever married anyone, they would marry each other. And now she's laughing and telling her editor, who is her pal.

What has to happen in the first scene is that all the information and much more has to come out. We wanted comedic beats about being a food critic, and we needed to show something of her personality. What kind of a person is she? What do we like about her? What do we know about her? What are her strengths and her weaknesses?

We need to show the same for George, her editor. Do we reveal that he's gay in the very first scene? It's a decision to make . . . because he is a very attractive guy who is of marriageable age, so we now know that he can only be a pal and he won't be an alternative love interest, but he has a different objective/perspective about it. What are we going to see? What's going to happen in the restaurant?

So I sat down to write scene one, and I began by reading all their faxes and then forgetting all their faxes. You don't want to be bound by any ideas that you've had before, and you get into the scene and you write it. But you're so well prepared and you've considered so many alternatives, and your emotions are already cooking over "I hate this idea," "I love this idea," "This is wrong, but it should be the opposite over here," or "This gives me a completely new idea I never would have thought of if I hadn't remembered that I once thought this but it should be this instead." Anything to get the creativity and the possibilities flowing so you're not just standing around looking at a blank page saying, "What am I going to do now?" You've got a million things and you're excitedly trying to choose among them.

SBK: And all this for a scene that's going to be how many pages long?

RB: That scene was probably rather long when it was first written. But I would have guessed that that scene would have been a four-page scene. That's a very long scene, four pages.

    Now, we write the first draft. We sell it to TriStar, and Jerry Zucker's my producing partner who's, of course, an incredible writer himself; P.J. Hogan, also a wonderful writer, comes on to direct; the studio has their feelings. P.J., Jerry, and I sit down, and everything begins to change and take shape and become a joint effort. The actors have feelings and opinions and it's a very collaborative, very time-consuming, process.

SBK: And so many of us are trying to get fewer voices of input sometimes.

RB: Well, that's a great question because here's how it developed. It developed out of a writer's frustration with the development process at studios. The development executives at studios are frequently very bright people, but as much as people want to pay lip service that you're all working together, you're really only partly working together, because those development executives have a lot of agendas. Of course they have the agenda that they want the best movie possible, naturally, but they have other agendas, too. They have to please their bosses. They have to show that they made a contribution to justify their Mercedes. After all, if they just read the script and say, "Wow, Ron's script is great. I wouldn't change a word!" Well, what do we need them for? [Laughs.] So they are forced, just by the nature of the job, to try to find things to change.

    And, of course, in any script, every decision you make could be made another way. So it's very easy to say, "Oh, I think everyone's too nice. They should be more angry," or "She should have told him off here," or

"I think it's unsympathetic that she did that." Those are cheap shots. It's easy to do that. And suddenly you're in an adversarial position because, although on the one hand, you all cooperatively want the best movie, nonetheless you're fighting against someone who can control you.

If the executive vice president of Twentieth Century Fox says, "Ron, I've heard your arguments, but I want you to change this. I want her to kill him instead of kiss him," eventually it's going to have to be that way, whether you quit and you don't do it and some other writer does it, or you want to stay on the project because you want to find the best way to do it. Eventually someone else is going to call the shots. The director and the decisionmaker at the studio will be the final decisionmakers and you will only have as much input as you can be persuasive.

What I realized when I hired the first person, Jane Rusconi, three years ago . . . was that for a writer to have his own development people is heaven, because then you have all these other voices, but you don't have to be defensive because you can say "no"—you're the boss.

Now you wanna hear other opinions because if you don't like them, you can say, "Sorry, Mimi. Sorry, Hannah. What you're saying makes a lot of sense, but I really prefer chocolate instead of vanilla." You're much more open to receiving stuff when you know that it's your final decision.

SBK: Now you're also producing as well. . . .

RB: Yes. Producing or executive producing everything that I do.

SBK: But still, you have to answer to a director and a studio.

RB: Oh, yes. Being a producer is not, as some people thought, to give you more control over the material. It just is a decision that I made with *The Joy Luck Club* that I didn't any longer just want to be a writer for hire. My original view of it was I was a writer; I wasn't a filmmaker. I loved writing the first draft.

But of course I cared. It hurt when there were changes that I didn't like, but I sort of had myself in a mind-set to feel "I'm a writer; I'm not a film-maker," and I tried to kind of assuage my feelings by walling myself up.

Well, it was just psychotic. It wasn't true. The screenwriter is a film-maker, even when he pretends he's a novelist or just a writer. He's one of, or she is, one of the very few most important people in the process of making a film.

So I began to say to myself, "I want to see the process through. I want to be part of the team. I have a big stake in who's cast in this. I know this woman 'cause I was this woman when I was writing her. I want to be at the rehearsal process because I know I have something to give. I want to be at the previews and I want to be at the editing process, because editing is simply rewriting in film, and I know I have something to offer."

SBK: You were an entertainment lawyer for all those years, but you were a novelist from practically birth, as I understand.

RB: Well, I wrote my first novel when I was two years old. [Laughs.]

SBK: Okay, seventeen.

RB: Yes, when I was a teenager I did write a novel and destroyed it in a fit of low self-esteem.

SBK: You wrote a whole novel and destroyed it? Like Richard Dreyfuss standing out on the Venice jetty in The Buddy System, *throwing his pages out to sea?*

RB: I wrote this novel. I was at UCLA before going to Stanford, and I had this wonderful English teacher and I showed her the novel. She was the only person I'd ever shown it to, and she said, "Oh, this is so good. Ronnie, you really have to write more. You really should be encouraged." I said, "Yeah, yeah, yeah, yeah. But can we get it published?" She said, "Oh, no. This subject matter is not appropriate. This is a personal fantasy of yours. You couldn't get this published, but you really have talent and, you know, you'll keep writing." So I went home and I literally burned, burned with a match, the only copy that existed.

SBK: Because she'd said you couldn't get it published?

RB: Yeah, because that was like the voice of God—this beautiful, brilliant woman who knew, who really knew, literature. How could I worship Fitzgerald and Faulkner and Dostoevsky and ever dream that I could do this? I'm an ordinary person. What a joke that I could really do this. So I went and did something related. I majored in Political Science instead of Literature.

SBK: What was the name of the novel?

RB: It became my first novel. . . .

SBK: So it eventually resurfaced.

RB: Sixteen years later, when my first marriage was breaking up, I was very depressed. I needed to do something to cheer myself up, and I began to rewrite that novel that I had burned. The same idea, the same character, but from a more adult and different perspective. It was called *The Perfect Thief*, about an art forger. And it was a love story and philosophical treatise on the subjectivity of reality, and I was never going to let anybody see it. But I had such a wonderful time doing it. My present wife, Chrissy, was extremely encouraging. We were just starting to see each other at that time, and she was very encouraging and that, of course, got me even more into it.

SBK: And at that time, you were pushing all these buttons for 360 files for eleven hours a day?

RB: Oh yeah. Practicing law full time. This had gotten written over the space of a year or two years in my spare time.

SBK: Early mornings?

RB: No. They were like on weekends or vacations or evenings or maybe an occasional early morning. I was negotiating the deal for Dick Clark's autobiography, and the editor, Jay Acton, and I become friendly over the phone. He says, "I'm leaving St. Martin's to become an agent, and I'd like to read this book you told me you wrote." I said, "Oh, no, I don't want you to read it." "Oh, Ron, let me see it." So I sent it to the guy. I'm terrified. . . .

He had to go to forty different places to get it published. If he hadn't done that, I don't know what my writing continuation would have been. But he did.

I think I got a $6,000 advance. The second one, *Lime's Crisis,* took a couple of years in the same way. But the third one, to tell you more than you want to hear, probably, I'd made an investment that had gone wrong and I was really kind of broke and I was very worried. So I got up every morning at 3:00 for two months and wrote a 110-page treatment of what *The Emerald Illusion* would look like, and that's how Predawn began. I knew that I had to do it in a concentrated way if I wanted to sell this for more than $6,000 or $8,000. I got an advance of $60,000 for that because I'd written this treatment. And that showed me that to really be a writer—not a dilettante, but a real writer—you had to do it every day. You had to get up every morning and just do it.

It sold for screen and I insisted on being a screenwriter or I wouldn't sell the rights for screen.

SBK: Well, that leads right into contracts. What goes into a Ron Bass contract?

RB: In other words, what can other writers learn from this? I wish there were generalities that could be helpful. There aren't. What you really need is to get a great entertainment lawyer to guide you and talk with you about what's important to you. Because what's important to one guy isn't important to somebody else.

I really have been lucky enough to be in a position where I could put some very strong things into contracts for myself, but you know, it's really very meaningless. For example, I have a clause in my contract for *My Best Friend's Wedding* that says I cannot be rewritten. Yet I was rewritten by P.J. [Hogan, the director] and even in one very wonderful scene at the end by Julia. The toast that Julia will give at the end of this movie was actually written by Julia herself, and it's wonderful. P.J. was very respectful and terrific to work with, but I was happy to let him collaborate with me in the writing process. Sometimes you realize on the set that certain things aren't gonna work.

I know I got in trouble the last time I gave an interview for the *WGA Journal*. I got in trouble with Joe Eszterhas who felt that I was too worried about the director's vision and not worried about the writer's vision. I've gotta be honest: we're making a film here, and if a writer wants to have his way, he should be writing novels where nobody can change your stuff, write plays where no one can change your stuff. But a movie is a collaboration, and eventually the director is going to have to make that work on screen. So, this is not to say, "Oh, the director is God. Whatever you want, please forgive my humble mistakes." That's ridiculous. Any director I've ever worked with would tell you I fight like a tiger for what I think is a better way to do something. But I do also understand that at the end of the day, there is this other guy. He needs to make it work, and if I enforced a clause that would make him unable to change lines I didn't want to change, it's a hard way to direct a film.

So, what the process is really about is not trying to get creative rights in a contract and enforcing them like an adversary. What the process really is about is finding and nurturing good relationships with the other filmmakers so that you're all working together. Yeah, you're gonna disagree, you're gonna be fighting and yelling and screaming at each other. I've certainly never made a movie with anybody where there weren't many, many heated disagreements. There have to be, because you care so much. But when there's ultimately respect and you know you were heard and you know that the guy is listening to you and dealing with the issues that you're forcing them to confront, the fact that he winds up writing the line a different way at the end of the day, I can't say that this is treason and capital punishment should be administered. I just don't think that's this business that we're in.

A Conversation with . . .

Horton Foote

If you know Horton Foote's work, you know it's not car-chase-laden. What it is, however, is a collection of stories about people trying the best they know how to make sense of their lives.

His stories, including plays, teleplays, and screenplays, have been written over a period of more than fifty years, and last year, at age eighty, he won a Pulitzer for his play *The Young Man from Atlanta*.

When he was a teenager, though, finishing up high school, he wanted to be an actor. "Passionately," he says, with quiet exclamation points. And started writing because he discovered it was a way to insure good parts for himself. The critic Brooks Atkinson took notice—good notice—as did others, and soon, by Horton Foote's admission, he became passionate about his writing instead.

And though he calls it tough on-the-job training, since then he's collected two WGA Awards and two Oscars: Best Adapted for *To Kill a Mockingbird* and Best Screenplay for *Tender Mercies*. And written a series of nine plays, called *The Orphans' Home*, which he's adapting for film, and about which college courses have been fashioned. And an adaptation of the William Faulkner story, "Tomorrow," which Faulkner approved so much he allowed Horton Foote to share the dramatic copyright.

The day before the Fourth of July, before his teleplay adapted from another Faulkner story, "Old Man," had won a Humanitas Award and before it had been nominated for an Emmy, he talked by phone from his home in Wharton, Texas about the compulsion to write, the long road it took for some of his scripts, and the value of keeping on.

SBK: You started out as an actor?

<u>HORTON FOOTE:</u> Yes, I did. A long, long time ago. I had finished high school and had just turned sixteen, and I told my parents I wasn't going to college and I wanted to be an actor. They, of course, were alarmed. They said, "Well, I don't think you're mature enough. You'll have to wait a year." Why they thought I'd be at seventeen any more mature than I was at sixteen, I don't know. But that was our bargain.

And I waited a year and said, "No, I'm not going to college," so they sent me to Pasadena Playhouse, which had a school at the time. And from there I was taken to the East Coast to summer stock and then I went to New York, and felt the need of further training. I began working with the Russians—Tamara Daykarhonova, Andreas Jilinsky, and Vera Soloviova. And then with the American Actors Company, I wrote a one-act play, *Wharton Dance.* We had a little theatre on 69th Street, and I played the lead in it. A New York critic came down to see it and liked it and liked my performance, so I thought, "Well, this is the way to get acting parts."

I went back to Texas and wrote a full-length play which they put on. And for some reason, word had gotten around that I had some talent, and at the opening of that was Brooks Atkinson, who was the dean of the critics, and Lee Strasberg and Clifford Odets, and a lot of theatre people, and the play was very well received. Much better received than my acting was.

And I thought, "I'm going to show Mr. Atkinson. I'm not going to write any more; I'm going to be an actor." But I went away that summer with the company and acted a number of parts, and all of a sudden, it just left me. I began to write. And I had a lot to learn, because I really had no preparation for it. So all that pain of learning on the job, so to speak . . . but that was really what started me.

SBK: What was the name of that first full-length play?

<u>HF:</u> *Texas Town.*

SBK: And was it a personal story?

HF: Yeah. Well, you know, all stories finally are personal in some way. I mean, they're all kind of collages of your experiences, don't you think?

SBK: I do. Although I was looking at a lineup of your movie scripts and thinking that probably Storm Fear *was not as personal a story.*

HF: No, no. The only thing about *Storm Fear* that attracted me was I've always been attracted to stories of young children under stress. And I think that's what drew me to that at that time.

SBK: But Texas Town *was a personal story?*

HF: Well, in a sense, but I would have to define what a personal story is. It's not autobiographical, if that's what you mean. It was a story based on what I observed in a time when I lived in this town at that period. In that sense, it was a personal story. But I wasn't a main character, even though I acted the main character.

SBK: What was it about, Texas Town?

HF: Oh, Lord, it's so long ago now—we're talking almost fifty years ago. Well, Atkinson was very extravagant in his praise of it. He said it was the epitome of the essence of a small town, which doesn't really tell you what it was about. It was the story at the time which I wouldn't subscribe to today, but this discontent at being in a provincial town and wanting to get away from it and seeing all the prejudices and the restrictions of life in a small town.

SBK: The plays that you wrote after that, a good number of them do involve other members of your family. . . .

HF: Oh, absolutely. Or variations. In the sense that I don't even know that they would recognize themselves or that people that knew them and loved them would recognize them. Again, they become kind of montages—you know, you take a little piece here, a little piece there, and you really create a new person. But they are based on observation and reality.

SBK: So how do you write about family without them all ending up hating you?

HF: [Laughs.] Well, I think that my family are aware of the fact that I'm very serious about this and not out to exploit anybody, and I'm trying to discover some truths.

SBK: Are you a fast writer?

HF: Yes, I am a fast writer, and also an obsessive writer. In other words, once I get started, I just can't wait till I get it all out and done. But then I've found it very valuable to put things aside for a while and then go back to them, when that kind of fever of creating has died down and you can be a little more analytical and critical in your judgment.

SBK: This ties in with something I was going to ask you before. You said you learned writing on the job. What sorts of things have you learned since then?

HF: One thing very valuable for me, and I didn't even know I was being given this gift, was that I was trained by the Russians. They have enormous respect for the written word in the play and the text. And they spent a lot of time instilling in us to respect that and to analyze the play in the sense of the through-line and the different beats and actions or whatever you want to call it. The motivations. So, in that sense, that was almost a way of learning play structure.

And, of course, I read a lot of plays, and then gradually you get to realize that a style is evolving, and in my humble opinion, style is not anything you can control any more than you can control your handwriting. It's very personal. Then what you have to do is nurture what has been given you, so to speak, and do the best you can with your given style. Because I think that dictates the kind of material you're attracted to and also the kind of writers you're attracted to.

SBK: Interesting that you mention the Russians and what they taught you about respect for the text and the written word. In your scripts, sometimes the actions seem very small on the surface, but they are revelatory of a lot going on underneath.

HF: Well, I think that, you know. There's a film I'm very fond of, I just looked at it again two nights ago, Tokyo Story, and to me, it's almost a classic in the sense of small actions meaning a great deal. And the same with The Dead, the John Huston film of the Joyce story.

<u>SBK</u>: *There's a scene in* The Young Man from Atlanta, *between Will Kidder and Etta Doris, which sort of echoes a scene, which is my favorite in* Tender Mercies, *with Robert Duvall and Ellen Barkin, when she comes back and he denies knowing the song in the same way that Will denies remembering Etta Doris.*

<u>HF</u>: Yeah. And then she forces the memory on him, kind of.

<u>SBK</u>: *Uh-huh.*

<u>HF</u>: That's lovely. I hadn't thought about that, but I think that's a very lovely observation, and I'm grateful for it. Because I feel that scene is very important in *A Young Man from Atlanta,* even though you wouldn't think in a conventional sense it had any meaning at all. But it has a subtextual meaning, I think.

<u>SBK</u>: *What appears to be a little conversation on stage or screen, there's a lot going on. So how do you know when you're writing that a scene you're writing is full enough?*

<u>HF</u>: Oh, I don't know. You have to trust instinct, I suppose. I don't think you can pass judgment on it till it's done. For instance, people ask me all the time why does Bob Duvall in *Tender Mercies* refuse to sing that song for that girl? I have no conscious answer for that. Just instinct told me to do it. In other words, I didn't consciously decide that.

<u>SBK</u>: *That scene makes me cry every time.*

<u>HF</u>: But you know, I wouldn't change it for the world. They ask me two things, they ask me about that and about his saying "I never trust happiness." And is that my personal philosophy, which it's not.

<u>SBK</u>: *Ah, yeah. I wouldn't imagine it was. Do you read your work out loud?*

<u>HF</u>: Do I read it aloud, after I've finished it? You know, sometimes I do. Certainly when I'm working on it, I do. One of the things that they've begun using today as a technique is that when a play is finished, a playwright will often get a group of actors and have them read it to him. I find that can be very valuable, depending on if you have the right actors.

SBK: Do you do that, in Texas?

HF: No, I don't. But I'm in New York often, and in New York there were all kinds of channels to do it. There is a thing called—I think it's called Radio Theatre of the Air. . . .

SBK: Is that from L.A., with Susan. . . .

HF: Loewenberg, right. And Robert Falls, who directed *A Young Man from Atlanta* at the Goodman Theater, is very fond of a new play of mine called *Vernon Early,* and he suggested this play which she read and liked and so we did it, and it was very helpful. Now I have a new play which I wanted Shirley Knight to do, and she just called the other day and said that she would like to do the same process, so in that sense I'll get a reading of this one, too.

SBK: So L.A. TheatreWorks did Vernon Early? *What's the new one called?*

HF: *A Coffin in Egypt.* That's not about Egypt, Egypt. That's about Egypt, Texas.

SBK: The multiple geographies of Texas. Not just Paris, but Egypt, as well. You do both plays and screenplays . . . when you do screenplays of your own plays, do you alter them?

HF: Oh, yeah. I mean, in the sense that you're in a different medium.

SBK: So how about The Trip to Bountiful, *which is another of my favorites?*

HF: Well, you see, in the movie was the first time we could take the trip. When it was first done on television, it was done when television was live, and they couldn't afford more than two or three sets. So the journey itself, you just had to dissolve and forget the journey and pick it up after the journey was over. And again on the stage we couldn't do it.

SBK: What was the evolution of that story? Was it a television play first?

HF: Yeah. It was a rather remarkable period for writers. It was when television was alive and there was a wonderful man called Fred Coe, who loved writers. And he didn't have a lot of money, he couldn't hire big stars, so he thought, "Well, I'll just gather some writers I like and feature them." So he got me and he got Paddy Chayefsky and Tad Mosel and J. P. Miller and Gore Vidal. . . .

In those days it was so close to theatre, television was, it was a very comfortable medium to me, and I really just ostensibly wrote about nine one-act plays which have since been published as one-act plays and done all over. And he would commission them. You'd come in and tell him a few things, and he'd say, "Okay, go ahead and write that."

It wasn't pitching in the sense we know it today, but you would just kind of share an idea and it was just simply to fulfill an obligation to the sponsors. I don't think he really cared. I think he would have said "Go ahead" no matter what.

I got paid the handsome sum of a thousand dollars to write *The Trip to Bountiful.* And let me tell you, in those days that was a lot of money, at least for this writer, it was. And we got Lillian Gish to do it. And Eva Marie Saint was in it and Eileen Heckart and John Beal. And I hadn't realized the power of television. The phones didn't stop ringing that night. Well, it was also a great tribute to Miss Gish, because, you know, she had fans all over America, and they just went wild to see her again. She was wonderful in it.

They asked me to enlarge it, and I did, into a three-act play, and we took it to New York. Then, for some reason, I felt very wedded to Miss Gish doing the part in the film, and for some reason Hollywood had the notion that she wasn't bankable. So I was offered through the years—I don't know whether they were willing to do it—"I'll do this if we can get Hepburn," or "I'll do this if we can get . . .," and I said, "No. I want Miss Gish." And that went on until Miss Gish had her 90th birthday, and even I had to realize that the part was too demanding.

And then Pete Masterson, who's my cousin, wanted to do a film. He was at Sundance, and I think Redford had encouraged him to do something he really liked. So he called me and said, "Could I try to get the financing for *Bountiful?*" And I said, "Yes, if we can agree on who gets to play the part." And he said, "Who do you want?" And I said, "Well, I want Geraldine Page," and he said, "So do I." So that was it.

But we had opposition to Geraldine, too.

SBK: Omigosh, and she seemed so right for it.

HF: Well, you know, that's hindsight. [Laughs.] But at that time, they had many other ideas who should play that part, and I just said no. I can be very stubborn at times, and I just said no. And sometimes I lose, and sometimes I win. This time I won. I just think she was extraordinary.

SBK: One of the first scripts that I wrote was a story about a young woman and an older woman. And I wrote it with Geraldine Page and Sissy Spacek in mind . . . but unfortunately didn't get to see it out with those two, but maybe we'll still get to see it at some point.

HF: Yeah. Don't ever give up on something. You just can't. Because you just never know. I mean, look. *Bountiful* was done in the theatre in 1954, and look how long it took. This is why I think that it's so outrageous that Hollywood still insists on holding the copyright for a script, because I think that the heart of the writer is the copyright, and controlling it. And I must tell you—I won't tell you who—but a very distinguished director/producer, after it was done on Broadway, offered me $15,000 for all rights in perpetuity to *Bountiful.* And I had very little money at the time and had a small family and small children. And my wife and my agent said, "If you do this, we'll never forgive you." So I didn't do it. And I'm so glad I didn't. But, you see, that temptation is always there when you need money.

SBK: You've done this adaptation recently for television—Old Man. . . .

HF: This was my second time at it—I did it first for Playhouse 90. John Frankenheimer directed it, and Geraldine Page played the lead, with Sterling Hayden.

SBK: Well, that's another interesting thing, because when you did it for Playhouse 90, I bet you couldn't set it in the bayou.

HF: No, we couldn't. In those days, they never went out for locations, so it was a whole new experience doing it at the river.

SBK: When you're working with producers, certainly I would think they would be wise enough to leave you alone to write a script the way you want to write it, but I also don't want to underestimate the ability of someone to say, "Mr. Foote, we really would like some more action in this scene." Do you ever get that?

<u>HF:</u> [Laughs.] Well, you know, I don't do that much. Usually what I do now is I either adapt something of my own, which they perfectly well know what's in there, or I've just finished an original, which is being done by Showtime.

<u>SBK:</u> *Is that* Alone?

<u>HF:</u> Yeah. Which was in the USA Film Festival in Dallas and is going to be in another film festival. And we're trying to get a commercial release for it. Showtime feels it's worthy of it, and they're giving us leeway to do that. And I've just signed up to do *Little House on the Prairie,* which is the first time I've worked with a commercial studio in a long time. But they are very supportive. They know how I work and what I want to do with it, so I don't anticipate any trouble.

<u>SBK:</u> *I wanted to ask you, too, about Southern stories. How do you think Southern stories are different from stories in the rest of the country?*

<u>HF:</u> Well, I think by what happens in the culture. I lived in New England for a number of years, and I was fascinated, interested, but I could no more write about New England than I could fly to the moon in the same way that I write about the South.

You know, there is a theory that what interests one as a writer is kind of programmed by the time you're ten years old. That doesn't mean that you're stuck there in time, but that your thematic interests are there. And certainly I think what you call upon subconsciously is fed by the place you live in and the people you grew up with.

The people, and I think the South for this period—it's diminishing now—but they had a real identity with a great oral tradition. They had wonderful storytellers. and, for whatever reason, they kept the history going orally.

And there were these enormous family connections and interest in the family and in the place. And then they were under siege so much of the time from many points of view—the different cultures at war with each other.

<u>SBK:</u> *You moved away, to New Hampshire, right?*

<u>HF:</u> Yeah, uh-huh.

SBK: And now you've moved back. And in the meantime you've won all kinds of awards, including a Pulitzer. How has that affected you?

HF: I don't think it has affected me very much. When I went for the awards ceremony, the guy who was making the address said, "You know, from now on, you will always be known as a Pulitzer winner. And everything that's written about you, that connotation will be there." There was the initial flurry when people were pleased and happy and a lot of congratulations, and then it dies down and then you look in *The New York Times,* and there are four or five plays that say they won a Pulitzer prize. And you go, "Well, it's nice to have it," but you just keep going. And that's my theme: keep going.

SBK: If people were to ask you what you do for fun, would you say, "Write"?

HF: I think so. That's my vocation and my avocation, too. I'm the happiest when I'm writing.

A CONVERSATION WITH . . .

Kasi Lemmons

You may recognize her as Jodie Foster's roommate in *Silence of the Lambs* or from her roles in *'Til There Was You, Gridlock'd, Fear of a Black Hat, Vampire's Kiss,* and *Hard Target,* but Kasi Lemmons has also been a member of the Writers Guild since '87, since shortly after she auditioned for *The Cosby Show* and Bill Cosby discovered she could write. Now she's written and directed her first feature, *Eve's Bayou.*

Based on a story she wrote several years ago, *Eve's Bayou* is about an African-American family in Louisiana, told through the eyes of the ten-year-old daughter. And it wasn't an easy road to getting it made. What's more, when things finally fell into place, she had just had a new baby, so she shot the movie with a three-month-old in tow. Now, though, she says Hunter feels very much at home on a set, thinking it a matter of course that 150 cast and crew members would greet him with a smile every morning.

And now Kasi herself is at home in front of the computer, having written several more features since *Eve's Bayou.* From Paris, where she was working on a script with her husband, actor/writer/director Vondie Curtis Hall, she took time out to talk about acting and writing and how it took *Waiting to Exhale* before backers finally began to acknowledge an audience for movies about African-Americans that were about things other than the 'hood.

<u>KASI LEMMONS</u>: *Eve's Bayou* was my first full-length script that I wrote by myself. I wrote it a long time ago. And since then I got to write a few before we got to make *Eve's Bayou,* but it was the first one I wrote by myself. I had written a project for Bill Cosby with two other women— that was in '87, I think—and then afterwards I wrote a project with a friend of mine.

<u>SBK</u>: What was the project for Bill Cosby?

<u>KL</u>: We called it *Tight Shoes,* and I don't think they ever did anything with it. He wanted three black women to write him a script. . . . At the time I had just been writing scenes for friends of mine to do in acting class.

I was an actress first, but I always wrote. I wrote even when I was a kid. And then around '86, I started writing short stories. And I had actually written a short story that was kind of part of *Eve's Bayou.* And I started writing these scenes for actors. The first class that I took in playwriting was John Ford Noonan's class at the "Y" in New York. That was my first formal education in dramatic writing.

And then in film school—at the New School—I made two films. One was kind of a docudrama which really broke form and broke the rules. . . . Some people really loved it, it did really well, but it pissed a lot of people off because I had a voice-over over this kind of documentary.

It was called *Fall from Grace,* and it was about homeless people in New York. I didn't know that there were rules to making documentaries, so I did a whole bunch of different things. We had talked to some homeless people on the street, and I had kind of composed a voice-over that Vondie read. And we had put this rap music over it and a lot of it was long angle shots of homeless people. And it was kind of controversial because of the voice-over.

The film did really well. *Comic Relief* used pieces of it, and it did a bunch of festivals around the world. For a seven-minute piece, I got some mileage out of it. And every once in a while, people would come up to me and tell me they were slightly offended by it because I had put this voice-over over this kind of heartbreaking footage. . . . But we didn't know— we thought it was cool. And I still really like that film.

Then I showed that film to Bill Cosby. I went in for an audition, and I said to myself, gearing up for the audition, "You know, if I ever get to meet

Mr. Cosby, I'm going to show him my film." And I don't know what I expected, but he said to me. "What I really need is a writer. Can you write?"

And I said, "Yes, as a matter of fact, I write scenes for my friends." And he said, "Well, write me a scene, and bring it in next week and show it to my head writer." So I came in the next Tuesday with my scene, which was perfect, 'cause that's what I was doing, you know—writing scenes. And he'd forgotten, of course, that he had told me that. He was totally not expecting me. But he gave my scene to his head writer, Matt Robinson, who hired me as part of a team of writers to write this movie for him.

SBK: Were you on the show at that point?

KL: No, I didn't get the part. But I got this writing job. And I guess it really changed my life.

Then I got *Silence of the Lambs* [as an actress], and the career was going okay. We moved to Los Angeles, and I wrote a script with a friend of mine, Billie Neal, who's also an actress and an extraordinary writer. We wrote a script together called *He Ain't Dead Yet*. And it was after that that I wrote *Eve's Bayou*.

I wrote it just for me. I was going to put it in a drawer and not show it to anybody. It was very personal. It was something I needed to experiment with.

SBK: In what way?

KL: Well, I thought I wanted to write a novel. And then I thought it would be fun to experiment with writing a screenplay as if it were a novel. So *Eve's Bayou* is kind of literary in a way. Then also I was experimenting with the type of prose. To me, it has a rhythm, like a long poem. So I was experimenting, and I didn't know if I was going to be good at it. It didn't occur to me to really show it to people.

I showed it to Vondie when I finished it, and he loved it, and he said, "You've gotta show this to somebody." So I showed it to my acting agent—I didn't know who else to show it to! And he gave it to the literary agent at the agency where he was, and that's still my agent: Frank Wuliger. Frank Wuliger really helped me set up *Eve's Bayou*. But I truly wasn't going to show it to anybody.

SBK: When you say it had a rhythm to it as you were writing it, were you fitting it into this rhythm?

KL: I didn't even try to make it fit into the rhythm. It naturally came out that way. But it was an experiment. I haven't really done the same thing since. I write poetry, really bad poetry—my mom writes great poetry—but it's almost like when you write poetry, you have a poem that kind of builds up inside you and then you have to spit it out, right? *Eve's Bayou* was a little bit like that. Like it built up inside of me and it just came out in a certain rhythm.

In a way, it's almost like now I would be more embarrassed to do it, because it was another time in my life when I wasn't concerned with the rules at all. Now that I'm kind of a professional screenwriter, I wonder if I might have been more self-conscious. . . . But I felt definitely liberated by the fact that I wasn't planning on showing it to anybody. I didn't care if anybody liked it. It made me laugh and cry. And I would sit there and cry and laugh, and that was really what I needed to get out of it, and I didn't really need anything else. All the rest has been icing.

SBK: You mentioned that it's personal. Were parts of it autobiographical?

KL: No, none of it is autobiographical. That's not really what I mean by personal. I guess it was a way of talking about a family. You know, I think that any writer who writes anything about a family, whether they're a novelist or a playwright, there are some elements of their family that are going to sneak in it, right? Or their best friend's family, or families that they've known, their cousin's family. So there are definitely parts of my family in it, but it's not at all autobiographical.

SBK: I don't know the Creole life, but this movie sure seems to be Creole life in all caps. How much of that world did you know about before writing it?

KL: I think I knew about it—it sounds goofy, but—in some sort of spiritual way. Because in fact I made it up. I was trying to have a story take place with all black characters and kind of liberate them to have made their own kind of town. That they were absolutely indigenous to this place where they owned the world. And they weren't necessarily feeling the weight of white oppression. Not that I'm not interested in that story, but it wasn't what this particular story was about. And I wanted them to be kings and queens in this. I knew there were places in Louisiana where the culture hadn't changed, or had changed in its own kind of interesting way, but places that had their own rules. So Eve's Bayou, I just made up this town that had its own rules and its own specific history, and that they were Creole.

And then late in the film, in preproduction, I sought out a Creole consultant—somebody who actually speaks the language, because it's a kind of lost language. . . . But you know what was interesting?

SBK: What's that?

KL: In preproduction I bought a book—I bought a lot of books for research—and I wish I could remember the exact title, but it was called something like *The Lost Negro People of the Cane River.* It's a history book. And in this book they describe this little town, right, up in the Cane River? And they tell this story that happened. This woman, I think her name was Maria Theresa, had a slave. And she became very sick with, like, cholera. And the slave woman saved her with a type of magic medicine. And the woman gave her the town. Or gave her some huge piece of property, which is exactly how Eve's Bayou gets started in my story.

So it was really weird. That's why I say, even though it might sound goofy, I think I kind of knew about it on some spiritual level that a place like this could exist.

SBK: That's always fascinating to read something like that after the fact.

KL: It was really weird. It was my production designer, we were sitting in the van on the location scout, and he started reading me this paragraph, and we all turned around, and it was hard for everybody to believe for a second that I hadn't read the book before, but I hadn't. I don't even think you can buy it outside of Louisiana. And it was just very, very interesting. Of course, that's my little history of Eve's Bayou. Jean Paul Batiste was stricken with cholera and the slave woman saves his life and he gives her that piece of land. And of course they begat the entire town.

SBK: How did you end up directing this film? You didn't start out directing it, right?

KL: I think originally I wanted to be in it. And then when people started really liking it . . . Oh, maybe somebody can actually direct this movie soon, you know, and my movie can get made! And that was pretty darned appealing. Then when that started getting more serious, I literally woke up one day on my birthday—I had already formed a partnership with Cotty [Chubb]—and I woke up on my birthday and I said, "I'm directing that movie." At the time we were talking about some very good directors whom I entirely respect, but I don't know, I woke up one day on my birthday and I wanted it. And I didn't want anybody else to have it. And I called my agent and I said, "I've had an epiphany and I must direct this—" And he's like, "Okay, okay, wait a minute." 'Cause we were already talking to all these people. . . .

SBK: You mean all these other directors who were thinking about it?

KL: Yeah. And it was the best birthday present I've ever given myself. I wanted it, and I didn't want anybody else to do it. . . . And when Cotty and my agent finally got over the shock that I had made this announcement that I was going to direct it, they took it very seriously. And Cotty said, "Okay, well, if that's the case, then we need to do a short, because I'm not doing a feature with you if you've never directed anything." I mean, I had made little documentaries in film school, but that wasn't going to get it, you know. So we made the short together—I think he was probably seeing if he thought I was a director at all and to have something to show people. But they supported me instantly. As soon as they got over the shock, they were totally supportive, and they always have been.

SBK: Tell me about the short. How short was it?

KL: The short is about twenty minutes long. It was a scene that I had cut out of *Eve's Bayou*. It kind of got back in later on, something kind of similar to it.

SBK: Which scene was it?

KL: There's a section of the film where Sam goes doctoring, and he has the little girl with him. And he goes and visits a lady, a beautiful sexy lady, [played by] Victoria Rowell. It's kind of that. That scene. But not exactly. Very inexactly. Inspired by that. It's just this little tiny, tiny piece and I made it into a full little film that has its own beginning and its own end, where a doctor pays a visit to a married lady.

SBK: Who did you use for your actors?

KL: I used my husband conveniently to play the lead. It's like, who can you get for free on Memorial Day weekend to act in your short? I happen to have extremely talented friends, so I'm really really lucky. Victoria flew back from France to do it. And Mike Beach, who's another friend of mine who's extraordinary. And this magnificent little girl named Kelli Wheeler.

SBK: You shot it over a weekend?

KL: We shot it over four days. We started on Thursday or Friday and we went until Monday. My agents lent me half the money.

SBK: That was my next question.

KL: And Cotty Chubb put up the other half like out of his bank account—so it was one of those labors of love. I mean, when I say I got support, I really got support.

SBK: That sure is. I know of Cotty from IFP [Independent Feature Project] West. How did he get hold of Eve's Bayou *in the first place?*

KL: Frank had sent the script to several people, and I had taken a lot of meetings. And one day he called me up and he said, "I've got this guy that I want you to meet. He's eccentric," he said, "but he's the man who can get your movie made." And I met him, and he was very passionate about the script, and he seemed to mean what he said and, in fact, he did.

SBK: In what ways?

KL: You know, a lot of people were interested in this script as a writing sample. They thought, "Oh, this is a really fascinating writing sample, but what I really would like is for you to write a script about *this*"—you know what I mean? But Cotty really wanted to make *Eve's Bayou.*

Eve's Bayou is one of these scripts that had a lot of fans, but people weren't just jumping over each other to make it. They thought it would be a difficult film to make.

SBK: Why did they think it would be difficult?

KL: An all African-American cast was the major reason. To make a small film that didn't have a lot of violence, that wasn't a street kind of "in the hood" movie with an all-African-American cast—kind of a new concept.

SBK: Pretty amazing, isn't it?

KL: It's amazing. But remember those articles about where everybody was surprised that there was a *Waiting to Exhale* audience? We're talking about an audience that people didn't know existed until *Waiting to Exhale.* Which is a shame, but true. So from where they were looking at my script, here is something that we all admire, but we can't figure out who is going to see this movie. So it was difficult for them.

SBK: How was Cotty different about that?

KL: Cotty saw it as a piece of art. He could isolate it. He could look at it and say, "I really like this, and I think this is worth making." I mean, he'd be the first person to tell you he wouldn't want to make a movie that nobody wants to see. But on the other hand, I think he's an idealist. He sees things as "This is something I would really like to see made." And I needed that, you know. We all do. I don't believe it would have gotten made without him.

SBK: That's great. It seems like you have a whole huge slate of projects you're working on or have been working on or have finished. Are these from people having seen or read Eve's Bayou?

KL: Yeah. Everything I got is pretty much because people saw or read *Eve's Bayou.* Right after I made *Eve's Bayou,* some of the first people that saw it were Michelle Pfeiffer and Kate Guinzburg, and kind of bravely, I think, they had me in for a meeting with Kate Guinzburg, and she asked me to write a script for Michelle Pfeiffer. I wrote a script called *Privacy* that everybody seems to like a good deal. It's totally diametrically opposed to *Eve's Bayou.* It couldn't be more opposite.

SBK: How so?

<u>KL</u>: Well, it's all white. And it's edgy, in a way. *Eve's Bayou* is kind of lyrical and slow, and *Privacy* is edgier. It has a different pace. It has a whole different rhythm. I love them both.

And I wrote a piece for Whitney Houston called *Eight Pieces for Josette* for Warner Brothers that we're hoping to do at some point. That's something else that I'm really proud of. It's about the classical music world.

And I wrote a movie for Cotty, actually, that I like very much, too. And now I'm writing a movie with my husband.

SBK: What is the movie you're writing with Vondie?

<u>KL</u>: It's for him to direct, and it's an adaptation of a book, called *The Impersonator*, by Diane Hammond.

SBK: When you actually sat down and started writing, how do you think your acting background influenced your writing?

<u>KL</u>: I wrote things that I wanted to say. When I wrote *Eve's Bayou,* I played all of the parts. And I wrote things that I as an actor would have loved to say. You know, "I'd love to have this monologue." "I'd love to say this line." And I think that acting and writing together . . . the natural marriage of that is directing.

SBK: What for you is the hardest part of writing?

<u>KL</u>: The solitude. I get lonely sometimes.

SBK: I understand this totally.

<u>KL</u>: Yeah. That's probably the hardest part. And then giving it over. You know, being a studio screenwriter and having to give it over. As a matter of fact, that's absolutely the hardest part. Solitude's nothing compared to that! Giving it over and letting other people give you notes on it. And they start telling you what they think the character would say or wouldn't say, and it's like, "You don't know, sonny! I made her up. How do you know what she would say?"

SBK: And have you gotten that so far?

KL: Oh, of course. I mean, it's a natural part of the process. Actually, it's an important part of the process. The mature part of me knows this. It's an important part of the process because making movies is a collaboration and it's absolutely necessary to get the feedback from people who are going to put a lot of work and money into getting the movie onto the screen. And so I appreciate the process, but I find it painful. And I'm sure it's the same with all writers. I don't think I have a unique position here.

SBK: Right. But how have you figured out at this point how best to handle those meetings, where someone is telling you something that you don't necessarily think is the best way to go with it?

KL: Wow. That's a difficult question. I try and talk them into seeing it my way. But if they're insistent, I try to make it work. I try to find a way of thinking about it so that it works. Or you try it, and you give it your best shot but maybe it doesn't work and then you go back to something that you suspect might work better. But I try to give it my best shot. Say, "Okay, well, I don't agree, but maybe." And I think that the best producers I've worked with look at it as a collaboration with the writer, as well. And they appreciate my point of view so that we can negotiate. And say, "Okay, well, you give a little, I'll give a little, and we'll come up with this, and maybe this will work for all of us."

A Conversation with . . .

Melissa Mathison

How do you start a letter to the Dalai Lama? Ask Melissa Mathison, writer of *E.T., The Black Stallion, The Indian in the Cupboard,* the miniseries *Son of the Morning Star,* and now *Kundun,* a movie about the Dalai Lama.

"You say, "Your Holiness, comma," she says. And then, "I think what you do first is you write his secretary, saying, 'I am enclosing a letter to His Holiness, and this is what it says, and would you please read it to him for me.'"

Ultimately His Holiness said "yes," and over a period of six years, Mathison met with him and interviewed him, both in the U.S. and in India, and never had to worry about checking her tape recorder because, as she found out, "he is a mechanical genius of sorts. He loves all that stuff. So he had to see what system I had. He kept checking it and readjusting the microphone—he liked it better when I had a little standing mike than the mike clipping on. So it was great—I always knew that I'd just put it on the table and he'd see that it was working!"

She not only had an idea to write a spec script about the Dalai Lama, but after she finished it, she had an idea to ask Martin Scorsese to direct it.

On a fall afternoon, just after returning from accompanying her son's class trip to Plymouth, Massachsetts, Melissa Mathison talked from her home in New York about how she went from that initial letter to finished script, and some about that other movie about a youngster from a foreign place, *E. T.*

SBK: You actually wrote a letter to the Dalai Lama?

MELISSA MATHISON: Yes. Between Bob Thurman and Richard Gere, I got his address in Dharamsala, India, where he resides, and sent a note to his secretary introducing myself and saying I had this idea to write a movie about the young Dalai Lama and did they think they might permit that. And I got a very nice note back saying, "It sounds very interesting. Could you give us some more detail?" So I wrote up a little three-page treatment that I sent off to them, and they wrote back again saying that His Holiness would be in California and would be very pleased to talk with me.

Just to get mail from India alone is pretty exciting, but then when it has the Dalai Lama's little emblem in the corner, it's really exciting.

SBK: I bet. So then you met him in California?

MM: Yes. I believe he was getting some sort of humanitarian award in Santa Barbara. So my husband and I drove up to Santa Barbara, and the next morning, when we went down to breakfast at the Red Lion Inn, we went into this huge giant room, and there were all these Tibetan men, in suits and robes, leafing through my treatment. It was like watching a teacher correct your paper—watching them make little notes, watching their faces to see if they thought something was funny—and they'd finish and put the pages back in their little portfolios and drink their tea. It was pretty nerve-wracking.

We waited our turn and met the Dalai Lama, and I'll never forget the first time I met him. It was all this beautiful California sunshine outside, and then you went into his room and it was very peaceful and quiet, and he literally came out of the shadows.

He held his hands out to us, and he has a remarkable, beautiful face. And Harrison [Ford] and I started laughing! I think it's the perfect ice-breaker for him, with his sense of humor, because people are so overwhelmed when they actually meet him.

His secretary was a movie buff, and so he was able to ask a few movie-type questions. And His Holiness said that it sounded like it would be a good idea; if I wanted to try [making a movie], that that would be fine.

Immediately after our meeting in Santa Barbara, we went up to Santa Cruz where he was going to relax for a couple of days, and that's when I began my series of interviews with him. I started by asking him questions about his childhood and what he remembered, what were his earliest memories of his home and his family. He's always so charming and accessible. One of the questions I asked him was to tell me a ghost story. I wanted to know what scared little children in Tibet. So he told me this very scary story that they had told him as a child, about some woman wandering around the monastery with a basketful of skulls. He said they told him that story to get him to stay in his room at night.

During that year I think I saw him again in the United States at some point, and interviewed him many, many times. And I'd send him faxes with questions that I wanted to be sure I had correct. His secretary would always send me a response. And then I finished a first draft that we took to India to present to him in '92.

SBK: What happened then?

<u>MM:</u> Harrison and I sat with him in his office and we read through it. Harrison was actually the reader, and I was the looking-at-the-face-and-seeing-how-he's-reacting person. He would stop and make corrections or ask a question himself or interrupt us because this had reminded him of a detail that he thought I might want to hear, or a couple of times he would stop and explain something about Buddhism to me, which was truly a magnificent privilege.

We spent about two hours a day for six days, going through the script, and it was great fun. We all cried at different parts, and at the end . . . I mean, I've been at read-throughs before, but this was unlike anything else! His attendants would be there, listening and smiling and pouring tea, and at the end we were all sort of choked up, as much for the finishing of the movie, which has an emotional ending, as the fact that this sort of encounter had come to an end, and it was such a special time for me, for God's sake. I think he enjoyed it, but for my husband and me, it was truly one of the great times of our life.

SBK: What kind of notes did he give you?

MM: He would be specific about rooms or prayers or outfits or ornaments, like he'd say what would be on the table or what his Buddha altar would look like at that stage of his life, what he had had on that altar, what his morning routine would be like as a ten-year-old boy, what he remembered about certain characters. Some of them had a stoop or a limp or always carried a handkerchief crumpled up in their hand. He had lots of little character details he would remember.

And then he'd sometimes just get into the subtext of that scene—why had I chosen that, and what did I want to illustrate with that? And maybe something seemed a little too frivolous or a little too personal. It was like really doing a biography of somebody, and they're surprised at what you find interesting about their life.

He found the format amusing, also, because it was in script form. So you've got your "INT-POTALA-MEDITATION ROOM-NIGHT," and of course it took him about two seconds to realize what all of that meant, but he was interested in the shorthand of scriptwriting itself.

One thing that was funny is we'd be reading a scene, and he'd say, "Ah! This reminds me. . . ." And he'd tell me a story, and I'd hold up my hand and say, "Keep reading—that's the next thing!" He was always one step ahead of me, and in fact that was usually what was coming up next, and we'd all laugh at that. He kept being humble and saying, "I won't keep interrupting," but we'd say "No, no." It was a joyous occasion to go through this.

SBK: I wanted to ask you about the structure for the script itself and how you decided what to include in making a biography of a whole entire person's life.

MM: Oh, God . . . I knew where I would begin, and I knew where I would end. And there certainly were monumental moments: the discovery of the boy, moving the boy to Lhasa, the death of his regent, the invasion of the Chinese, the visit to Peking, the meeting with Mao—I mean, there are these huge moments.

Those were the big blocks, and then it was a matter of making sure that all the little bricks between big blocks would be building character and history along the way. And always staying personal and in the first person with the Dalai Lama.

So in some ways it was harder, and in most cases it was easier, because the audience—the writer—was allowed to know only as much as the boy did. So if things seemed a little obscure or confusing, that's how they would have seemed to a six-year-old boy. As he grew older, things became clearer, and the details of political life and the dilemma of Tibet all became more explicit because he was of an age where he could understand these things. It was a nice style for me to use because it helped me leap over some bits of information and stay with the very personal, whereas if you try to truly tell the story of the epic history of Tibet for twenty years, you know, it'd be a fifteen-hour movie.

So the personal point of view helped a lot in the structuring of it.

SBK: How'd you decide to send it to Scorsese?

MM: When I finally had a script I was ready to show, other than to my close friends, I met with my agents, and they had this list of directors. It was pretty funny to go through this list: "Oh, maybe," "Oh, no," "Oh, yes". . . like they'd be interested, you know!

But the person I wanted to send it to was not on their list, and that was Marty Scorsese. Everybody thought I was nuts, and I know I was right. And now I really know I was right. This was my greatest piece of intuition on this movie, to send it to Marty, because he actually did want to make it, and of course has made just an incredible movie.

SBK: What all went into that intuition?

MM: Well, first and foremost, if you're going to send it to a director, you may as well send it to the best director! Why not? So there's that. But Marty, I knew, was interested in the spiritual. We know he had worked in the world of religious biographies and spirituality. I had actually met Marty a couple times. I was an ex-Catholic and he was an ex-Catholic, so we'd talk about our nuns and priests, and there aren't many people who are interested in the world religions, and he was, so I assumed he would be interested on an historical level.

But more than that, this is a movie about a personal destiny, and about taking on the word and absorbing it and living it and choosing to not only let it guide you, but when things become impossibly difficult, to not turn your back on what you know. And I think that's what Marty's movies are always about.

SBK: In what way did he have input on the script?

MM: Well, once he said he wanted to do it, which was the next most exciting moment of this movie, we would get together as often as we could and sit down, start to go through it, and start to talk about it. He is the most gentle and humble of teachers, I'll tell you that. He didn't say, "This is fine, but this scene stinks." I mean, so polite and so cautious and careful and not deflating you as he gets you to make the changes that he needs.

We just talked it over and over, and we talked through the characters and we talked through the meaning. It was always about "What is the meaning of this movie?" It's not a gangster movie, it's not a mystery, it's not action, it's not romance—there was always an underlying meaning that certainly neither of us had ever striven to articulate in any way. So it was fun having the essence of the movie grow as we worked on it.

And we would play with letting it breathe on a horizontal plane as well as a vertical one. We experimented with stepping outside the walls which surround the boy and seeing the world through other people's eyes. None of those things worked; we eventually did go back to the first person narrative, but in cutting back to the original decision, we learned so much. . . .

And it improved on a cinematic level, because that's the way it has to be written for him. He has to know what he's going to shoot. We'd have this great discussion about a twelve-year-old boy in a room, and we would go on for two hours, amusing ourselves, but finally it would come down to "What is the shot? How do we tell it in moviemaking?" So it was distilling all of our bigger thoughts down to a photograph.

He's so visual . . . and he's also incredibly uninhibited in moviemaking. There are no rules for him like "If you're here, you can't go there.". . . He doesn't stop himself from saying, "Oh, we're not allowed to do that." And that was really a great experience.

SBK: Can you think of an example in the movie that was enhanced by his lack of rules?

MM: Well, we had dreams already built into the movie. His Holiness told me his dreams and we used them in the movie because it was a more direct way to get into the mind of this boy. But then Marty did something with the dreams, like there'd be exposition within a dream. I mean, whoever heard of that? Or there'd be the inexplicable cut to a dream— you didn't have to show the boy falling asleep. He always assumes the intelligence of the audience and is so aware of how quickly the audience's mind works, so we could make a visual leap that in any other world people would need to set it up and then to explain it, and he doesn't feel the need to do those two things. We'd leap into a dream and use the dream to satisfy an expositional need, and leap out again, forward in time, assuming that the consequence of that exposition would have been understood. And that's really exciting stuff.

SBK: When you were writing this, did you realize it might be a dangerous movie?

MM: No. Well, I'd had enough association with Tibetans and the Dalai Lama at that point to know that all he has to do is get up in the morning and they consider it dangerous. He scares the Chinese to death, and rightfully so. He's a man of peace who, after forty years, they simply have not been able to beat out of the brains of the Tibetans. The Dalai Lama has never made a step that the Chinese have not been there before him, giving orders as to how he may be received or demands on a government that they not receive him with any protocol or let him do this or let him do that.

So I had witnessed this. And I felt in the back of my mind that they certainly would not be pleased once they heard about this movie. I was surprised that it took them so long, and then I was surprised at the boisterousness of their complaint. Telling Disney that they should shut down our movie—that's pretty loud criticism, and it's also culturally misguided. But it was not a goal of mine to kind of get that reaction. It is not written as, and was never conceived as, a political message movie. That's the last thing in the world I would want to write or the last thing in the world Marty would want to direct. It just is the story of this boy.

SBK: Are you a Buddhist?

MM: I wouldn't dare say I'm a Buddhist compared to the people who really have definitive practices, because to be a Buddhist is to practice. I just met this great rinpoche, Sogyal Rinpoche, who wrote the book *The*

Tibetan Book of Living and Dying. And he told me that what I was was a word I can't remember, but it means that you are a Buddhist in that you are a student of the nature mind, which is the core of Buddhism.

SBK: What do you think accounts for the current fascination in this country with Buddhism?

MM: I don't think there is one. Certainly there are people who are listening to or looking at Buddhism as a philosophy of life, as something that can help you get through on a very personal level. But I don't think there's some big movement going on, as [the media] would have us believe. I mean, you know what? If there was, we'd all start to notice life getting a little bit nicer.

SBK: I want to ask you, too, about E.T. *and how it came to be.*

MM: I was with Harrison on *Raiders of the Lost Ark,* and halfway through the shoot, we were all in Tunisia, and Steven Spielberg asked me if I would be interested in writing a children's movie about a man from outer space. And I thought that sounded like a really wonderful idea. And that evening, he and Harrison and I drove across the desert all night and talked about it: what would he be like, when would he come, where would he be, what would the family be like, what would the movie be about, those kinds of things—kind of a wonderful discussion. And then we all returned to Los Angeles, and I started writing. And once a week I would visit Steven in his editing room and we'd go over what I had done, and we'd chart out where we were going and talk story, and I'd go back and write some more and come back again. So we did that for eight weeks, and there was a first draft.

SBK: So "E.T., phone home," that's your line?

MM: Yeah! All the lines are my lines. But it certainly was never considered to be anything very special at the time of the writing. Actually there was a big discussion about whether he should talk. As I remember it, I called Steven one day and told him that E.T. was starting to talk. And he said, "No, no, no, we agreed. E.T. is not talking." I said, "No, I know. You're right. We agreed, E.T. is not talking. But he's actually starting to talk." So "Okay, you better come in."

And I said, "Look, I think it can work." We decided that it actually could work to let him speak very little, but he could never say anything he hadn't heard. And he had heard "phone" and "home," because the little girl had said, "Do you want to phone somebody?" And Eliot had kept saying, "Home, home, this is your home." So he had to put a sentence together, and that was what he came out with.

SBK: I have to tell you how one of your movies affected my son. When he was five, we took him to see The Black Stallion. *And with that opening scene, where the father gets killed in the shipboard fire, he dived under the seats and we had to take him out of the theatre. . . .*

MM: [After *E.T.* had already been playing a while,] [producer] Kathy Kennedy and I decided we should go one Saturday afternoon to the Cinerama Dome and see what it was like. So we went in, and it was an amazing phenomenon because it was sold out, for starters, and you're surrounded by a whole roomful of people. And there were all these little children who, as E.T. was dying, were bursting into tears and clinging to their mothers, grabbing their necks, weeping, and mothers patting them, saying "Everything will be all right."

And Kathy and I were thinking "What have we wrought? Is this a good thing?" That was a pretty amazing experience.

SBK: Have you gone on the E.T. ride with your own children?

MM: Oh, years later—I think we only did this three or four years ago— my kids decided they wanted to go to Universal, so we went there, and I had, being a part-time Hollywood mother, known enough to call ahead. I did say, "We'd like to go on the E.T. ride, and I hear there's a big line, so can we be sure we get on?" Something like that. So we got to the ride, and when you go in, they ask you your names, and as you exit the ride, two of ten riders will be said "goodbye" to by E.T. So when we got off the ride, they did say "Goodbye, Melissa," "Goodbye, Malcolm," and "Goodbye, Georgia," and it was actually one of the great moments in my kids' life that their mother's friend E.T. had seen her, said goodbye to her, and somehow knew about them. My son was too old to buy it exactly, but he did like the ride, and my daughter totally fell for it.

SBK: And one more thing: do you still write to the Dalai Lama?

MM: I send him faxes now. Not every day or anything, but when China was asking Disney to shut the movie down in Morocco, I was writing him a fax about once a day, because I thought he would be so amused by it, sending him Xeroxes of the stories. Because for him, he literally works on a different plane than we do. And his feeling is that your enemies are your gurus, because they teach you to be a better person. So all of this, I'm sure, was terribly amusing to him, the huffing and puffing over this silly little venture in the Moroccan desert, trying to re-create his life. I'm sure he did find it very amusing.

A Conversation with . . .

Atom Egoyan

Funny how our writing often reflects our thought process.

Take Atom Egoyan. In person, he does what characters in his movies sometimes do. Big spaces often sit between his thoughts. Spaces in which you have to listen, wanting to figure out just what it is he's going to say next. Wondering what it is that's going on in that space.

And then, when he talks, it's often in a big stream overflowing with ideas, multiple ideas per sentence, things it's clear he's been thinking about for a long time. He's also self-assured enough in his thoughts that he's willing to be open about his vulnerabilities and the paths his work has taken and is taking him.

Growing up in Victoria, British Columbia, he really was named Atom by his parents, and was writing and making movies all along, including four short films as an undergrad at the University of Toronto. He even, at one point, was in a plane crash, and filmed the whole thing.

Along the way he's put together a string of movies which are distinct, writing and directing them all. His eighth, *The Sweet Hereafter*, which he adapted from the novel of the same name by Russell Banks, took the grand jury prize at Cannes this past year.

He lives and works in Toronto with his wife, Arsinée Khanjian, a member of the informal company of actors who often populate his movies. From a mixing studio in Toronto, where he'd been mixing *Sarabande*, a project with cellist YoYo Ma based on the Bach cello suites, Atom Egoyan stopped to talk about *The Sweet Hereafter* and how it fits in with his other projects before and after.

SBK: Your wife gave you the book first?

ATOM EGOYAN: Yes. In some ways, the project begins with two gifts. My wife actually gave me the gift of the book itself for my birthday, I think, about five years ago, and I just was completely bowled over by the scope and the detail of the story—the ability that Russell Banks had to give urgency to the most banal aspects of these people's lives and the way he was able to create this sense of a moral universe within this one community.

And I felt that it was the first time I read material which had similarities in some ways to my own films, but also was a huge leap ahead in terms of the maturity of the piece and the challenges it presented. I was at a point where I really wanted to surprise myself, and I was convinced that it was the thing to do to try and see if I could honor and serve the spirit of the book and also make it personal.

So the second gift was that I got the option. And that gift was the result of meeting Russell and convincing him that I would be the right person to try this adaptation. I also promised him that I'd be able to actually make the film. I think one of the things that was frustrating to Russell was that all of his books had been optioned, and he's a huge film buff, but he'd never been able to see the screen version of any of his work.

Because I work independently, and after *Exotica* I was quite certain that I could raise the money for this, I promised him that I would make the film. And we talked about the fable-like qualities, and how important it was to make sure that the film could operate at that level. So I then began working on the adaptation of the story.

SBK: You said that Russell's book is similar to things you've done, which I agree. It's similar in its perspective about human beings, and the stance of the narrator is similar to some of your work.

AE: And also the level of discourse it provokes with the viewer in terms of having to question their relationship to time, and having access to the experience of how characters apprehend events, as opposed to just looking at these events in a passive way. That, to me, is a really important part of how I construct movies.

I can look at two scenes in *The Sweet Hereafter* which, I suppose, illustrate this. The scene of incest between the father and daughter in the barn, where up until that part in the film, you're not sure what their relationship is; you might think that he's an older boyfriend. And then you see the scene of him in the barn, and the way it's presented is from the perspective of what a young woman who's involved in that sort of relationship would have to imagine in order to somehow preserve her equilibrium, her psychological equilibrium. She'd have to think that this was a romantic gesture. And I think very often when you see an incest scene, it's shot from the point of view, and it's written from the point of view, of that character, as we understand the nature of the abuse and the violence of the abuse reflecting back on it. But the reality is, at that moment, she would have had to believe it was something else.

So it's a very challenging and complex idea, but it was important for me to situate the viewer in the middle of that and to see what she had to see at that moment. The effect that that has is that we almost sublimate that scene, we forget about it until the very end of the film when she confronts her father, and the father denies the relationship and can't even begin to talk about it. And at that moment, as she mentions in the script, "Do you remember, Daddy, you were gonna build me a stage lit with nothing but candles," the viewer then will retrieve that scene in much the same way that the character would have to retrieve her whole experience of the relationship. And that type of moment, and that type of passage, is really crucial for me. It's why I make films.

There are certain properties that are inherent in the presentation of moving pictures. We believe in a reality, we want to believe that what we're seeing is actually happening. And rather than succumb to that, I love the idea of challenging that and playing with that, and by doing so, maybe entering into the subconscious of my characters and having access to that.

The other scene is the scene of the accident itself, where Billy views the bus crash through the ice. Again, that scene would normally be covered from so many different angles. What was important for me, in the way I wrote and executed that scene, was to see it as Billy would have seen it, within that one frame. Maybe I am talking too much about directing than writing, but it's written that way in the script, too. It's very clear that this is from a static frame, and we actually see what Billy sees, so that later on in the film, he talks about "I was behind the bus, I saw it happen," and we can revisit his experience of it, as opposed to just looking at that moment as an event. We understand it as an experience.

And right after that, we go back to the image of the sleeping family, and we begin to hear Mitchell Stevens' story of his own catastrophe with his daughter. To me, the structure of a film is a question of preparing the viewer for what they need to receive and understand in terms of the underlying psychology of what's happening to these people. And that sometimes means making a choice not to follow linear presentation.

This film had a much broader appeal than *Exotica*, because all you need to know if you are ever confused is that it's about a community before and after an accident. That's all you really need to know. I mean, all the other time periods are really irrelevant at some level besides that huge sense of before and after. *Exotica* was much more abstract in the nature of its construction.

SBK: The book is written in four segments, Rashomon-*like, in a way. When you went to pull it together into a screenplay, what was your starting point?*

AE: What I began with was what it means and why we need to tell stories. What you get in the book are four first-person narratives, and they are written almost as depositions. That form has a huge significance in terms of the film, because it's ultimately through a deposition that a character is able to find redemption. In the book, these stories are being told to the reader, and there's something quite plaintive and quite straightforward about who they're addressing. It's a literary device, a first-person device, and an attitude that we expect and understand as a reader.

But in film, it's a tremendously difficult thing to translate, because you either use voice-over, which is not something that I'm accustomed to, or you have to find somebody that they can address their ideas to within that community, and that meant some degree of reconstruction and contrivance.

The most difficult character, or the one I found most interesting at first, was Mitchell. There's nobody in that town that Mitchell could speak to, that Mitchell would make himself that vulnerable to, I felt. So I created the notion of this airplane trip, being on a trip to visit his daughter and sitting next to an old friend.

That was actually, in some ways, one of the first things I did. And that got me really excited, because I thought, well, this is interesting—here is a major part of the film in another public carrier. I mean, the bus is obviously something which transports this community, and the future of this community. I really do believe that children represent the future, and so every morning, the future of this community is transported in this bus, and I felt that it was very interesting to contrast that with this plane, which is another transporter. . . .

SBK: and another closed stage . . .

AE: And another closed stage, so I felt that there was an interesting thing to parallel and to structure the story around in terms of weaving back and forth from the airplane to the community. So you could almost say the first instinct was almost a sculptural one, of finding a way of positioning and telling the story that would allow me to move back and forth in time, much like the poem, which came afterwards, but allowed me to actually comment and to remove myself from the community while enhancing the ideas I was working with in it.

It's all the people that are repositories of somebody else and the responsibility you have when you carry someone else's history. So to have this other character, Alison, who had a memory of what his daughter was like, and confronting Mitchell with that, was to me a very provocative and identifiable circumstance.

I think we've all been in that situation in an airplane, and it's almost a device. It was funny to see *Private Parts*, where that's sort of used as a framing device in that movie, too. [Howard Stern] gets into an airplane and sits beside a woman who hates him, and he basically defends himself by the end of the trip, which is also intercut within the film. It's a place where you are forced to speak, you're forced into a relationship. What I found interesting about that choice was that here's a man who insinuates himself into a town, and forces himself into these people's houses and into their rooms so that he can get them to speak and get them to believe in what he has to present, and suddenly the tables are turned and he's in a situation when he has to speak to this young woman who is confronting him, asking questions about his daughter, asking questions about his past.

And in a way, there is a sense of how we can heal ourselves by talking about our experience and our circumstance. And by revealing the truth, and by sharing a truth, and by delineating what the truth is, we come to some sense of resolution. And that is a very important thread in the film, so anything I can do to enhance and emphasize that was really helpful.

In the case of Billy, because of who Billy Ansell was, there wasn't really anyone he could talk to. He's someone who keeps to himself. So what we're prepared to accept as a literary device had no meaning, really, in film convention. I decided not to have him speak to anyone, but his story would be told in a greatly simplified way.

With Dolores, she tells her story to Mitchell as he comes and conducts the interview, and that was in some ways the most straightforward.

Nicole was a challenge, because I seized on the idea of the Pied Piper and that would serve as her narrative, and yet I felt that I needed more. So I did create a voice-over in an early draft in which she is talking to Mitchell in her imagination. We get a glimpse of that in the end now, when she sums up and she is speaking to Mitchell. But in the first rough cut, we had a voice-over which wasn't working at all. As inventive as I thought it was, it was actually thunderingly banal and reductive. But the advantage was that I shot these close-ups of Sarah Polley, anticipating the voice-over, and when I took the voice-over away, I was left with these extraordinary images which I wouldn't have shot otherwise, so I'm very thankful that I wrote the voice-over, because it meant that I had this coverage of her, including these very slow dolleys onto her face, which I probably wouldn't have dreamed of if I hadn't thought there would be voice-over over them.

Ultimately it's a story about people constructing narratives. And that became a very interesting device in the film. Because the most extraordinary gesture Nicole makes, when she's in the middle of this deposition when she's supposed to tell the truth, she suddenly finds a way of controlling her own narrative by lying, and thereby empowering herself.

So even though the seeds for Mitchell's story are laid, she's able to disrupt that and give herself dignity in the process.

SBK: You mentioned earlier about Allen Bell and the Pied Piper. The Pied Piper doesn't appear in the book, but it provides a real interesting visual metaphor for the story. How'd it happen, and who's Allen Bell?

AE: Well, when I first showed my first film, *Next of Kin*, in a small theatre in Victoria, British Columbia, [a man named] Allen Bell came up to me, and the things he said about the film were just so lucid and inspiring that I felt that I would like to work with him. He's a poet, he was a lit professor for many years, and he is now living in semi-retirement. He's just an extraordinary resource. He's somebody that I can trust to be unblinkingly honest about my work and he likes to sculpt my scripts. He likes to take out any extraneous words. He likes to make sure that everything is reduced to what is absolutely essential. I resist that sometimes, because I think in the process you might take away some of the character of the piece, but he's a great person to work with. It's a wonderful relationship that way. And he is absolutely clear what his responsibilities are, and he has a tremendous amount of respect as to what I will do as a director, but he has an unflinching belief that the script is paramount, and he wants it to be in its best shape before it goes before camera.

SBK: And what exactly happened re the Pied Piper?

AE: I went, as I often do, to tell him what I was doing next. And as I told him what the story was about, he said, "I think we're about due for a modern version of the Pied Piper." And I just got goose pimples and rushed out to get my tattered version of Robert Browning's poems, and it was such a gift! It was just so amazing to see how the ideas of that poem— the themes of a village that loses its kids, the idea of a person who comes in promising to solve the problems of the town and not getting a reward, and the themes of annihilation and punishment—all those are woven into the poem and found resonances with Russell's story. So it suddenly gave me, also, a sense of authorship.

I think that was very important to me, having written seven films based on original material. I needed to feel as though this was something which, at a certain point, I could become the author of in spirit, and the poem in some ways gave me that angle and that point of entree.

SBK: And it worked beautifully.

AE: It's uncanny how well it works. The only thing I had to do at the end was . . . I felt that with her lie at the end of the deposition, I wanted to make clear that we all knew she was lying, so I invented some poetic text based on Browning's rhythms at the very end of the poem, which was intimidating, but I think it works.

SBK: Do you remember the lines?

AE: Yes. "And why I lied, he only knew, but from my lie this did come true, those lips from which he drew his tune, were frozen as a winter moon." It's so bizarre because I'm in the lab, mixing another movie, and they are playing the film in the background. The moment I said that, I heard the flute of the Pied Piper coming from the other room.

SBK: One of the things I've noticed about your work, and this is probably more a directorial comment than about writing, but you allow silences between the words.

AE: Yes. I can't tell you how frustrating it is sometimes, and they won't do this with this movie, but with the other films, sometimes the criticism is that it's removed or that it seems I've sucked any emotion from these people. And I've always found that really frustrating because to me there is nothing more emotional than what is unspoken or what is repressed and held back. Very often the journey that my characters find themselves in is getting to that point at which they can actually identify their emotions because the circumstance or fate has robbed them of the ability to express and has taught them that they need to hold back. That frustration and that desire to find communion is really what fuels a lot of the drama in my original stories.

I think in my earlier films, especially, I was so intrigued by the emotions that were kept back—the things that people couldn't say. That came from, I suppose, my theatre heroes, like Beckett and Pinter. I've always loved the silence and pause where there would be extended moments where the viewer or the reader would have to imagine what was unsaid. And it made you aware of how frail the process of communication is.

In many films, one of the things we love to amuse ourselves with is how effortlessly people can communicate with one another, and very often, in real life, there are moments of hesitation and uncertainty. Part of our job as screenwriters is to construct dramatic situations which warrant an exchange of words and ideas, but I still think that when we can define those moments where people lose words and don't know what to say, and trust that that will be as dramatically convincing as a barrage of sound being emitted from someone's mouth, that that is a way of accessing people's interior landscape.

So a lot of it has to do with working with actors, because when you choose to work that way, you have to rehearse and make sure the actors know what it is they're suppressing and what it is they're not. But it's also in the script itself. One of the characters in *Speaking Parts*, Lisa, a character who's returning a videotape at one point, is obsessed by this man she works with who's an extra. And when she's admonished by the video store owner [for being] obsessed with someone who's an extra, who doesn't have a speaking part, she retorts by saying, "Well, there's nothing special about words." And maybe there isn't. Maybe ultimately it's how words can sometimes convey a feeling and sometimes they can't. And I'm just as interested in those moments when they can't.

The difference between the characters in *The Sweet Hereafter* and my own [earlier] characters is that all these people in this town know who they are, they have a very clear sense of how they are rooted in this community. That's thrown into question after the accident, but they always are able to refer to what they were. In my other films, I think people's experiences have been so shattered and fractured that they are in the process of trying to understand what constitutes their own identity. The viewers aren't allowed to identify with any of my other characters because [the characters] don't even know who they are, and you are much more aware of what it is they need to do in order to piece themselves together. Those films are about finding that moment, and finding a sense of discovery. In *The Sweet Hereafter*, it's very different. The characters are identifiable, they are very vivid, and we see them through their darkest hour, but we understand and are given enough idea of what their routines and their habits and their relationships are that we can invest ourselves in them in a more direct way.

And that was something I needed to do. I really felt like I was getting tired in some ways of my own way of drawing characters. It seemed as though I needed to learn more about what a novelist does, and this was a great, great experience that way. I don't immediately want to go back to one of my own scripts, and my new project is another adaptation.

SBK: Sarabande? *Or another?*

AE: Oh, no. I just signed with Icon to do an adaptation of *Felicia's Journey*, by William Trevor, the Irish writer.

SBK: So you didn't want to go back to one of your own scripts right away?

AE: Not right away. I just think that I'm entering a period in my own development where I am very open to collaboration. So with this experience I had with YoYo Ma where we spent a lot of time talking about what it is he tries to do with his art form and what music means to him, and listening to him, I created this drama, or a comedy, based on a number of circumstances that happened around a performance of the suites. You know, someone in the audience begins a coughing fit, and the tension as to whether or not he should interrupt or keep playing; a master class he gives with a very troubled student who had to give up her cello to become a doctor; and then intersections and parallels in all these different lives—all that was a response to listening to YoYo and hearing what he felt, and trying to interpret that, and collaborating with him on this unique project.

The operas, I had an incredible charge last year when suddenly I had the opportunity to direct *Salome,* which is, I think, a totally forgotten play by Oscar Wilde, and maybe in some ways it makes a better libretto than it does a play, but suddenly to interpret that material and to interpret it in the context of Richard Strauss's music, that was just so thrilling and so educating. I felt that I was apprenticing myself to these other people's visions, and learning from them and applying my own ideas.

I've been involved in a number of art installations which have also had a high degree of collaboration, and my next opera projects are both new operas. One is in London at English National Opera, with the English composer Gavin Bryars and the poet Blake Morrison. It's an adaptation of a Jules Verne short story called "Dr. Ox's Experiment."

The other one is an original libretto that I've written, called *Elsewhereless*, and I'm working with a Canadian composer here for a presentation in 1998. In opera you work very closely with a designer, so I'm working with this extraordinary theatrical designer, Michael Levine, and we're coming up with a concept for "Dr. Ox's Experiment" together.

I think for so long in the early part of my career, up to *Exotica*, I was just really concerned with making sure that people understood what I had to offer, making sure that people understood what my voice was. And with the profile and success of *Exotica*, I felt that I could loosen up on that a little bit, and perhaps develop my own talents by working closely with other people.

A CONVERSATION WITH . . .

James L. Brooks and Mark Andrus

It takes a lot of guts to call a picture *As Good as It Gets*. And, in truth, it wasn't the first title of the picture. The original title was *Old Friends,* and the logline read something like "Three unlikely people become friends."

Yet this picture, with such an unlikely log line, written by Mark Andrus and James L. Brooks, was voted Best Movie—Musical or Comedy at the Golden Globes, and was nominated for Academy and WGA Best Original Screenplay awards.

Jim Brooks created, or co-created, characters on TV and film who've become a part of our vernacular: Mary Tyler Moore, Lou Grant, Rhoda, the characters on *Broadcast News* . . . and he's had a hand in, either writing, producing, or directing, a whole host more: *The Tracey Ullman Show, The Simpsons, The Critic,* and others. But *As Good as It Gets* began as a spec script, from a writer named Mark Andrus. And I was interested in finding out more about how they created this movie, and had audiences—okay, me, for starters—both laughing and crying in the same movie.

In the days following the Golden Globes, and before the WGA and Academy nominations, Jim Brooks and Mark Andrus sat down, in the tradition of their partnership on *As Good as It Gets,* on different

days, but on the same lot—Sony—and talked about the part this script played in their lives.

SBK: How did you get a copy of this script to begin with?

JAMES L. BROOKS: Marc Platt [then president of TriStar] and Stacey Snider [then president of production at TriStar], I think, sent it to me. And it knocked me out. And Mark was one of those voices that I responded to, as a producer. Mark had been through a billion years of studio notes, and was pretty worn out, having done gorgeous work. And it is in the nature of Mark that his earnestness and his heart is so great that he gets you to suspend disbelief. It's in the nature of me that I'm very practical, and I've gotta motivate everything and I've gotta understand everything, I've gotta believe everything, and my fanciful streak is not so hot. So Mark had really been exhausted, I feel, and I took it for what I thought would be a polish, as a producer. In that polish, I got lost. I got lost in respecting what was there, I got lost into personal stuff, and almost a year later, I was still writing.

SBK: What do you mean by lost?

JB: Into it. Very into it. Not a producer assisting it. Crunching on what I perceived were the problems. And respecting what Mark had done, and somehow, I think the two of us formed this extraordinary alchemy, because we're very different, and yet we each did personal writing and poured our hearts out, so that we ended up, I feel—and I think he feels, as well—being a real team.

And we're an unlikely team, and I think it's an unlikely film, but everybody's heart was in the right place, and somehow . . . you know, you can get mystical about it. But I'm very privileged to have worked on the script.

SBK: What was it that you saw in that first script?

JB: Just something I respect and was willing to support. It's very different as a producer than a director. As a producer, what you have to see is a writer you're willing to support. As a director, you're going to have another year and a half of your life, and you've gotta have a great sense of mission that's personal and visceral—I think! I think!—in order to not be full of shit.

SBK: And when you were reading it, even just to produce it . . .

JB: Great characters and great earnestness. Which is not, I think, my long suit, but in other words, love of character. I think that was it. Love of character. And it was very tender. And it was very different and similar to the final picture.

SBK: How different and how similar?

JB: The heart stayed in the same place. Lots of the words were the same. The tone was changed, the emphasis was changed. It was a very romantic script that I struggled to make real, and finally, I'm one who believes that if you can make things an out-and-out comedy, man, you know, try! So that happened, too.

And also I identified with these characters. Mark created these characters, but Melvin I have a great sense of identity with. Simon I just researched my tail off. I spoke to artists. I spoke to gay friends I'd had for years and asked them questions I never thought I'd ask any human being —"You ever get a hard-on for a woman?"—just things you don't ask. I had long conversations about promiscuity and about what romantic love is in the gay community. Stuff that you'd never go into, but I think you can't be smug when you do a screenplay. You can't say, "Well, I have the politically correct attitude about gays, and therefore I can do it." Now it's your subject. Now you have the responsibility to find the truth. So I had lots of those conversations—blushing through most of them, by the way.

And Carol, who was there. Oh, there was a big change where I gave Melvin a clinical illness. He didn't have a clinical illness. He was that way, but I made it clinical. So that meant all the research on obsessive-compulsive disorder. And Carol, who had an ill son in Mark's draft . . . I knew a working single mother who had a child with the illness we finally did in the picture, and I knew what she'd been through. So I had that to study and be true to. And then Helen [Hunt] visited with the same woman and spent time with her so that we were rendering something. Again, it was just the effort to make things true and real. And if an actress spends some time with a woman in this spot, it's a sense of responsibility, too, that you get. And I had a sense of responsibility to it. I think it took me a year because I respected what Mark had done so much. It was like, for me, loving *Terms of Endearment* as a book and feeling beholden to McMurtry.

It was that kind of journey. And because Gracie [Films] is about respecting the original writer, it would have been horrendous if that original writer wasn't fully represented at the end. And he was, I feel. We each plunged in and served it. He was the one who started it. And then we each plunged in and served it. And it became king, not either one of us. But he was the one who first thought of it.

SBK: You were talking about the tone a little while ago. When you were writing it, how on earth did you know it was going to be funny?

JB: I always believed that they'd laugh when the dog went down the chute. I believed in the nervous laughter of that moment. We added the woman to give an attitude towards the audience. But this is what makes writers nuts, and this is what can put you in bars, telling sad stories the rest of your life: it was so vulnerable.

There was, in all our minds—certainly in my mind, and certainly in Richie Marks's mind, the editor—a scenario for disaster. This character was so horrific. My game plan, God help me, was the audience would sit there, "I hate this man, I hate the Sony Corporation, I don't like this movie, I'm thinking of lea . . . wait a minute!" Because every time everybody learns the same rule, I just stop liking the rule. Like when everybody knows comedy should be fast and puts out those stopwatches to make people talk faster for comedy, I say, "Well, wait a minute—what's the alternative?"

And people talk about character arc, this thing that may or may not happen in life. But what I hoped here is that there would be an audience arc—that these characters might move a little, but the audience would move in their full understanding of them.

One of the things that happened in the research, this guy Eric Fishel, a great contemporary artist, talked to me about working with a model. He was the one I got a lot of that stuff from about being the observer. And there was a line that finally got into the script that said, "If you look at somebody long enough, you discover their humanity." And I hope that was the ride for the audience. There are indications early on to hang in there, you don't know the full picture—which is why the guy's clinical illness helps—and as you hang in there, something else starts to happen.

SBK: Hang in there with Melvin?

JB: Hang in there with the movie and Melvin. This is what I really believe, that if you changed any of the four actors in the top four parts, the picture not only couldn't be the same picture, it couldn't get to first base. I think if anybody but Jack [Nicholson], Helen [Hunt], Greg [Kinnear], and Cuba [Gooding, Jr.] played those parts, you couldn't get to first base. Cuba, what he does is . . . as the movie is least accessible, he is there with all his charisma and magic on the screen, somehow giving you some trust that it might be okay for you. And I really believe nobody else alive could have done the part and given us what Cuba gave us for that part. And then, of course, Shirley Knight was extraordinary, but I think literally we couldn't have gotten to first base without those four actors, which is again what makes writers crazy.

SBK: I'm still curious about knowing what's funny as you are writing it. Because the Melvin character is one of the vilest I've ever seen on screen, and yet we laugh. We're shocked, and then we laugh.

JB: There was something very freeing in this guy who's off all charts. Mark had created a guy who was fun to write. And I'm somebody who enjoys writing long speeches. There was a writer I worked with on *Lou Grant*, Leon Tokatyan, who used to love writing long speeches, and I just dug it. And I'm a huge admirer of Paddy Chayefsky's work. There's this theory about screenwriting, you gotta be terse. "Underwritten is king." And I always love if you can pull off speeches. God knows, you yank a lot out if you direct 'em, so put 'em in there. And this guy was fun because it was to me part of his ailment that he talked in these rants.

So there was his first thing with Simon, where he just goes off, and his thing with the Hispanic maid where he just goes off. There were other instances where he went off that were pulled from the movie, but that was great fun.

And I remembered working with Bob Moore, who was the director of *Boys in the Band*. He directed my first full-length piece, a movie for television, so I knew him quite well. He was the first person I ever heard of who died of AIDS. *Boys in the Band* was the landmark gay piece—nothing was like it—and he told me the story about how opening night, the author came to him and said, "What if they don't laugh? My God, what if they don't laugh?"

And Bob's answer to him was, "They've been laughing at sissies for two thousand years. They ain't stopping tonight."

And I had Bob's voice in my mind, because there's, God knows, the homophobic stuff, and it does finally play funny. You can't be sure it'll play funny, especially in today's climate, but I had Bob's voice in my mind on that.

And what ended up is the question about tone which I hope and think is in the movie. And God, I don't know how much I'm supposed to say, but I'll just tell you everything that's true that I know about it, because I'm still discovering the movie, because the movie was so humbling for everybody who came in contact with it. It was just so hard and so impossible and so frustrating and there were so few days when you were thinking you'd nailed it, and I was so much the naysayer, and there was so much "If you do this, it's too silly," and "If you do this, it's too dramatic," so you're always saying "no" and you're always looking for something you can't describe.

I think there are some key moments. One of the most important things was just a little piece with the Neutrogena soap in the bathroom. Because that is the big clue to suspend judgment on this guy for a minute. There are those elements of Melvin that, instead of looking at him like a freak, at a certain point we reach a critical mass of information about him that gets us involved with him. And that's the big deal, because the kind of laugh he gets in the second half of the picture is very different from the kind of laugh he gets in the first half of the picture. And Jack is magic in playing it. Jack can move a muscle in the second half of the picture and get a laugh. The scene in the car, where we're telling a rough, earnest story on the part of Simon, and there are just a few cuts to Jack that make it still live as a comedy scene . . . And that was the deal. Basically, the first part of the picture, we're just taking out all our fishing licenses and we're trying to get the audience to give us permission to be funny and to be serious.

I think the seminal moment is when he goes into the restaurant. There's a certain kind of black comedy going on in the picture up to that point that is okay, that is surviving. You know, it's getting some laughs, this black comedy. And then there seems to be more of it in store when she says, "You're going to die with ordering this breakfast every morning." And he says, "We're all going to die soon. It sure sounds like your son will."

And that kind of thing has been black comedy up to that moment, and then she takes it super seriously, as somebody would, and I love it because it's like seeing your parents fight. It's just such a horribly uncomfortable moment to witness, because he has blundered into such a perverse intimacy with her, just blundered into it. And she tells him off as few people have been told off.

I had a friend who argued with me and said that that character would never use "fuck" as a noun. She would just never do that. And I think it's just so important because what it did is it crossed some kind of boundary, and she had to cross a boundary to let us know that he had crossed that kind of boundary with her. So I think it's the most important moment in the picture, because once you go from that moment to her stupid date, and start getting that kind of laugh, I think then the picture has all its licenses in order. And once people permit you to do that, and they can no longer predict your tone from moment to moment, they've started to give themselves to the movie.

I think the other crucial occurrence was we went to film the hospital scene with Simon as a dramatic scene. It's the most dramatic thing in the story. His face is all carved up, we have to see it for the first time, and it was written with some delicacy to try and get some laughs, but honoring the seriousness of the moment. And when we went to film it . . . I think we're still truthful, I hope it was still well observed, but just the idea of going that far out with it, it happened on the set. I think it was very important for the picture, because the great thing that happens after that first moment is that his face is rough to look at, and he hasn't seen himself yet, so he's going to see himself through their eyes. And we decided to play it comic.

I think it's still truthful, but the last moment again, after playing it pretty comic, pretty broad, the last moment is quite serious, and the audience goes there. So it's at that point, the willingness to take those turns is just an extraordinary part of what we're doing, and what we're doing can't succeed unless they're willing to take those turns.

SBK: Speaking of the audience, I know you do a lot of testing. It's in I'll Do Anything, *but I've heard that you pay attention to the audience. What are you looking for when you do audience testing?*

JB: Well, first of all, I come from television, where I had an audience. I hated testing in television; I think it was inaccurate in television. The *Mary Tyler Moore* pilot tested terribly, *Room 222* tested terribly, and I really had bad experiences with it. But when I did movies, the stakes are so high, and the testing is so vital to how they treat you, that it seemed from my first movie that I directed that the only way to deal with it was to embrace it. Because if you said, "Ah, I hate it," you're in such conflict, and you've gotta be willing to see whether you get laughs or not, so you're testing it just on that basis.

We changed our title because of the test. It was called *Old Friends,* which I never quite understood. But we had a very terrific first screening which took all the weight off our backs, and we're feeling euphoric and we're floating out of the theatre because we had been so fearful of a disaster and it went so great. They had these focus groups—they picked 20 people out of the 500 to see the movie—and the focus group had been wonderful. We were on our way out and everything was great, and one guy in the focus group, as he's putting on his coat, says, "Gee, I'm glad I saw the movie this way, 'cause I'd never pay to see a movie called *Old Friends.*" And the other people went, "Yeah, yeah, you're right." And I got whiplash looking back into the theatre.

And you know, why go against that when you learn that?

We learned we were funny in testing, and then I felt they were laughing too much and we were becoming trivial. So the battle was to put resonance in the picture, in letting people know we meant it. Because the emotional life of this picture was enormously important to Mark's and my intention, and they were laughing so much, to the point of making it a lesser film, I thought. And we worked to correct that.

Hans Zimmer was the one who kept on saying to me, "You want more emotion. Don't stop." And we kept on going for our intention.

We also learned that having gotten them to go with the movie, the one thing they would not accept was convention. Finally what they expected from us was to keep on trying to be true and to keep on taking turns. You know, you can't switch your game once you get them to buy your game. So the ending became tremendously challenging.

And we ended up with them going into the bakery. And then that started to mean something to me, because it's true to the illness, too. With the illness, distraction is one of the things that helps you not be a slave to the illness. This guy was distracted by a lot of good stuff. So that he inadvertently steps on a crack when he kisses her. And then he inadvertently steps on a crack as he enters the bakery and notices it.

What I do feel good about is that what these two people earned at the last moment, is an utterly mundane, carefree human moment, of which there had been precious few in their lives, you know? A carefree moment where you're just smelling a roll, it's sort of visceral, you're with somebody with good will, you're not on guard, you've gotten to some place, you have a feeling of well being, you're in a bakery—and man, what a journey to get there. What a journey to get to mundane and simple.

That journey, of course, began with a spec script written by Mark Andrus, a screenwriter who started out a while back to go to law school and got sidetracked by writing. The characters in his stories, and subsequently his scripts, got noticed by people at UC Riverside, and then the USC writing program, and before he finished the USC program, he already had an agent. Mark lives down in San Juan Capistrano, and a week after the Golden Globes, he drove up to L.A. to talk about this script's beginnings and his own.

SBK: What was the origin of this script?

<u>Mark Andrus:</u> I actually was in a jacuzzi, which is the only place I get any ideas at all, late at night. And I suddenly thought that I wanted to write a story about the vilest man in New York City, that lives across the hall from a guy that he can't stand, who is a gay artist. And that was it. That's all I knew. I don't storyboard or make cards or anything, and I usually have no idea what it is beyond a simple idea until I sit down and start writing.

And it just sort of evolved. Carol evolved and her son evolved and there's not too much rewriting. The first draft is pretty much straight through at two or three hours a day, and maybe eight or nine weeks.

SBK: Without three-by-five cards or anything?

<u>MA:</u> No, I never . . .

SBK: You just barrel through?

<u>MA:</u> Yeah.

SBK: The Melvin character really is one of the vilest characters I've ever seen on the screen. Was he funny, as well, at the time you were creating him?

<u>MA:</u> The thing that amazed me is I didn't realize. . . . I don't go to films much, and so I have no idea what audiences actually laugh at, because everything that I see is either rented or on satellite. And I just watch it alone and I react, but I have no idea what audiences react to. So the first preview of this movie in San Diego was the first time that I realized that even things that I thought were meant to just simply shock got big laughs. I mean, this character was an isolationist. He was afraid of people, he didn't like people, and so he used words to drive people quickly away without having to interact. He didn't like to touch people or to talk to people. So I would write things that I didn't think were that funny but were meant to shock, in a sense. And they got big laughs. I think that was the most surprising.

And then somebody said, "Well, you also have to look at how Jim Brooks sets up a shot. He sets it up for the laugh." And it's really true. He's writing even in his directing. It's so brilliant the way he can set you up for something that you don't expect, and then it is funny. Whether shocking or not, it is funny.

<u>SBK:</u> *I wondered as you were writing, what you thought we were going to think of this guy, because he's so terrible. And yet I could remember only one four-letter word, though Jim assures me there are three.*

<u>MA:</u> There are three. In the original script there were many, many more. He actually toned it down and in a sense romanticized it a little bit more. I think he warmed the script up.

<u>SBK:</u> *In what way?*

<u>MA:</u> I think he made Melvin more understandable. We had different outlooks on what Melvin was, and my outlook was more you didn't really have to understand him, but ultimately you had to relate to him and slowly come to accept him. My tack was more that these people slowly broke him down and slowly brought him back to life, and so it was the interaction and connection, the love that he grew to have toward Carol, that made him better. That made him a better man.

And I think Jim wanted the audience to understand that this was a man that could get better by taking a pill. That first of all, you knew what was wrong with him—he's obsessive-compulsive, he says it in the office, where before nothing was ever said about what he was. He washed his hands a lot, he locked the doors a lot, but if you knew what that was, then you knew what that was; if not, you just thought it was a strange characteristic, I guess.

SBK: Jim alluded to the fact that you had gone through a bit of a mill before the script got to him.

MA: We went through incarnations. The first incarnation was [director] Mike Newell, who's phenomenal, and I had met with Dustin Hoffman at one point and did a rewrite for him, and then he left for, I think, *Outbreak.* Then Kevin Kline was attached for a while and he left to do *French Kiss.* That's how long ago this was. And then Laura Ziskin left to run a studio, and Mike Newell left to do *Donnie Brasco* . . . gosh, probably something before that. I don't know; it's been so long.

SBK: What are your first drafts like?

MA: They're simply writing, and the characters kind of inhabit. Although I've been told I have some characteristics of Melvin, I think that they exist without me, other than I'm writing them. The story tends to tell itself when I write. When I'm not writing, I'm not thinking a lot about what I'm going to be writing the next day. I'll write the two hours, or three hours a day, and then that's it.

SBK: Funny, walking down the hall with you, I had no indication that you were like Melvin. But you've been told that?

MA: In the sense that I'm very much an isolationist. I'm very anti-social. For years I had extreme anxiety, panic disorders. So other than using language to keep people away, which I never do, but being by myself is very much a characteristic that I share with Melvin.

SBK: We know some of the story of Melvin, but how about you? Did you always set out to be a screenwriter?

MA: Not at all. My brother, who is four years older, was a poet. He was an English major and he wrote short stories and he wrote poetry, so I totally avoided that going through school. I have a bachelor's degree in economics;

I got my master's degree in business administration. And I applied—I was twenty-two or twenty-three—for law school. I had two quarters to kill, and I took my first fiction writing course ever at twenty-three, and it was like, "Wow, this is fun." And I got a lot of encouragement.

SBK: Where was this?

MA: At UC Riverside. At the time, the chancellor there, Tomas Rivera, was a published author and a poet, and he had an advanced course in fiction writing. You would go up individually, one on one, once a week— you would write a short story and he would critique it. And he'd meet with you for an hour, two hours. It was great. For someone with no self-confidence, it was something to go up there and hear that you're doing something good.

And from that, he knew the director of the USC M.F.A. program in professional writing, and he said, "Why don't you just go down and meet with the guy and apply? If you get into law school and you want to go to law school, that's fine. And if you decide you want to do this, that's good, too."

And so I did, and I got into the USC program in writing, and I thought, "I can always go back to law school." This was so new and I enjoyed it so much that I just decided to go through it. One of the screenwriting professors there, Ken Evans, gave one of the scripts that I had written for his class to Bob Wunsch, who had just been fired from Universal for *Heaven's Gate* and had decided to start up his own agency again. I wasn't out of school, and he wanted to sign me for six months, and I thought, "This is great. If he can get me a job, that's great."

And soon after, Norman Lear, who at the time owned Embassy Pictures, signed me to a three-month contract that turned into three years. I still have no idea why Norman kept me for the three years, because I don't think I was that good a writer. But those three years were what gave me the self-confidence and the learning experience—to be paid to learn how to really write and to build up enough self-confidence to survive—otherwise I'd be back in law school and I would have been a lawyer. Because just the amount of criticism that you get on an everyday basis is fairly horrendous, especially when you're young and have nothing done.

SBK: What do you think you were writing that caught their attention in the first place?

MA: I think that it was the characters, but back then I truly had no idea of structure or story, and so it was maybe some fairly decent characters running through a mess of a script. And that's what I think the three years with Norman gave me. Just by practice, by writing scripts, you begin to learn structure.

SBK: And after Norman Lear?

MA: Norman sold his company, and then the offshoot of his company, basically, was Castle Rock. I worked for three or four years for Castle Rock, developing movies. I wrote one called *Late for Dinner* that actually got made, a small film.

And I'm working for Laura Ziskin now, for going on three years. I love to write under contract because of my fear of unemployment. I have this enormous fear of unemployment.

SBK: So you're under contract with Laura Ziskin? I know this is a completely naive question, but tell me how that works.

MA: It's actually very good, because I can present her with anything that I find or have, and independent producers that are free to come in and work with Fox 2000 can do that, or they develop and option a great many things, so they're offering me things based on what they have available, and it's just a meeting of the minds of what I'm best to write and what I want to write. And in the meantime you get monthly checks, which is perfect.

SBK: So do you send her what you're working on, or . . . ?

MA: No. Right now I'm working for Trevor Albert and Harold Ramis's company doing a project, an unpublished book that they optioned, and they have a deal with Fox 2000, I guess. So I just go off and write it and turn it in, pretty much unread except for me, which is like the most frightening thing of writing. I don't have other writer friends or I don't have family members that I give scripts to, so other than my reading it after I've written it, it goes to the people that have paid me a lot of money to write it. And it's frightening.

But I've had the good fortune of working with people who have great taste and are very gentle. Even if they don't like something, you don't get completely torn down. They're all encouraging people.

SBK: Way back, when Norman Lear liked your initial script, how did you work it so that he then put you under contract instead of just buying that script?

MA: You know, I'm not sure I have the answer to that one. Norman Lear was one of the few people, I think, that actually sought out young writers and would sign them to, like, a year contract, to give them a chance to write. I think it was like a goodwill gesture. Certainly there's a hope that maybe one of them will write a great script, but I don't think that was the point of it. I literally think that he wanted to give young writers a chance to write and learn how to write, and that was my first experience with being under contract.

Once that was there, and I understood how comfortable that was, I continually sought out contracts, over the advice of I think every agent that I've ever had. Contracts tend to limit you, because you're not free to take any project, so you're limited to the studio that you're under contract with, generally. And your salary generally is slightly lower, because if you move from script to script, you can increase a little more rapidly as to what you're paid. But I don't think there's any equivalent to the comfort factor, so that's worth whatever loss there is. So I became very comfortable with the contracts, through, I think, Norman's gift to me.

SBK: And with Laura Ziskin, she read one of your scripts? Is that how that relationship began?

MA: Exactly. She was an independent producer at Sony TriStar, and she was given *Old Friends* four-and-a-half years ago or so, and she immediately optioned it and started developing it. And when she went to run Fox 2000, I said that I'd love to work with her, and she said, "That sounds good," so we started a two-year contract, and then I just renewed for another year. She's one of the best producers to work for, as far as her loyalty and dedication to writers. She's great to writers.

SBK: So you get paid bonuses for your scripts that you write?

MA: Yeah. I think the overall contract figure is against all the things that you write. You still have individual prices for each script that you write. So you can actually supersede your contract level, and then they pay you more. But for every movie that's produced, there are still the bonus aspects to each movie. So it's basically a bottom-line figure, and I've had contracts where I haven't earned my guarantee. But hopefully you always want to out-earn your guarantee. But that means maybe two scripts a year, and sometimes I'm down to like one-and-a-half scripts a year, so sometimes I don't get the guarantee.

I can't think of anything better than having that comfort level. I really like that.

SBK: Getting back to As Good as It Gets, *when you saw it on the screen, what were some of the things that pleased you about it?*

MA: Almost everything. Every single line was as good as I thought it ever could be or better. It was just where you're totally shocked that what you thought could be is at least as good as that, and probably better. Because other voices and other ideas were added to your ideas, and it just made something that was so good to see. I was so overwhelmed by even the rough cut. I tend to get very distracted, but they invited me to see it on a TV, and they had all the numbers and the times running above and below, and there was no music and a lot of things were missing—it was a real rough cut—and I was just sitting there in love with what Jim Brooks had done to this. I mean, that part of it—you have no idea what it's going to be—you write it, and then I had no contact with Jim during his rewrite process, and then filming, I was on the set twice, so I didn't have a lot of contact with seeing the film done and seeing the process. And then I saw the film. And I'd kind of forgotten about everything. I'd forgotten my script. And you see it, and it's a life that is existing on screen there, and that was great.

SBK: How do you know when you get one of your ideas and a character is good and when it's perking for you?

MA: It's usually when I barely understand the character. I'll be writing and if they say things that even surprise me, then I think it's working. There is another kind of space that you go to, and so many of my characters say things that I think I wouldn't think of, ever.

SBK: Can you give me an example?

<u>MA:</u> Well, with Melvin, a lot of it, especially in the first drafts, is just the vileness that he would attack people with. It was really, really strong. And I try so hard to ease the uneasy situations and try to make people feel comfortable, and he was so antithetical to that, that I never would even think of saying those things or some of the lines that he would say. So it's like that, where they truly are unique characters, where I think that they're very little like me, then I think maybe they're working or that they're worth listening to. If I want to listen to them, maybe other people will.

<u>SBK:</u> *In the original, did Carol and Melvin get together at the end in the way that they do here?*

<u>MA:</u> They got together in a couple different ways. One was on the roof of a building where they end up dancing for the first time. The odd thing that I found is that when I watched it, I couldn't tell which was my writing exactly, and which was Jim Brooks's writing. And that shocked me, but I've read things that I was sure I had written, and then I've gone back to old scripts looking for it, and I couldn't find it. And there were things that I was sure that I hadn't written, and then I read an old script and it was there. So for me it's a great compliment that the person who adapted *Terms of Endearment,* which is the year I started writing and was highly influential in how I thought would be best to write in my career, is somebody that tends to write somewhat like me, where he can meld what I've written into what he writes, where I can't tell the difference.

1998

A CONVERSATION WITH . . .

Sherman Alexie

"Sherman Alexie" may not sound like your standard-issue Native American name, but my guess is Sherman Alexie is not a standard-issue anything.

A self-described "kid from the rez," he's already amassed critical acclaim for his seven books of poems, two novels, and book of short stories. The collection of short stories, *The Lone Ranger and Tonto Fistfight in Heaven*, won a Pen/Hemingway citation for Best First Fiction, and *Smoke Signals*, the movie he wrote from several of the stories in it, won the Audience Award at this past winter's Sundance Festival.

The movie's essentially a buddy movie, about two young guys, Thomas Builds-a-Fire and Victor Joseph, who leave the reservation to go to Phoenix. Thomas is a storyteller and the narrator of the movie; Victor's a basketball player. Sherman Alexie says he's "70 percent Thomas, 30 percent Victor—a jock-geek." He's also an office-supply junkie, a book lover, a husband, and a father of a one-year-old son.

The week before he was to leave for the Sundance Directors and Screenwriters Labs for his new movie, *Indian Killer*, which he'll direct as well as write, he stopped to talk about the parallels between poetry and screenwriting, *Smoke Signals*, and more.

SBK: This movie [Smoke Signals] *gives us a look at a part of life I wouldn't have seen otherwise.*

SHERMAN ALEXIE: That was the plan, to make a movie about Indians as we really are—the way we talk and act and look and think. And that's never been done before. Even many of the feature films, the smaller films, documentaries, etc., done by Indians always focused on the same sort of subject matter—it was all these highly politically charged films. And certainly this movie has politics in it, but we wanted it to be a basic human story.

SBK: Yeah, it's about real people. And I think there probably is a message in it, but it's not a message movie at all.

SA: No, no, no. That's all subtext.

SBK: So let me ask you the first of all questions, 'cause I'm your basic Anglo, who was brought up to say "Native American." And I notice that the phrase is not even used in this movie.

SA: Indians call each other Indians. My friend Roger and I were talking about this—he's black—and he said, "Black people don't call each other African-American."

SBK: So how do you like to be referred to?

SA: Spokane/Coeur d'Alene.

SBK: Spokane/Coeur d'Alene. Got it. Smoke Signals *was adapted from some short stories in your book,* The Lone Ranger and Tonto Fistfight in Heaven. *What was the hardest part for you of adapting your short stories into a film?*

SA: Well, it's a whole book of short stories. There are twenty-two linked stories, so the hard part was finding which events to use. I treated the book essentially like I didn't write it—I had no problem with compressing time or characters or mutating events, but the hard part was deciding which events to steal from other stories.

SBK: What did you finally decide?

SA: It ended up being four stories—the baby falling was a whole different character in the book, not Thomas. I went for the big dramatic events, like the party itself that caused Arnold to leave, and then certain stories that Thomas tells, like the Arnold protest story and the frybread story, are all taken from different stories in the book. One of the ways in which I integrated other elements from other stories is having Thomas actually tell those stories, which not only made him a storyteller, it also enabled me to use more pieces of the book.

SBK: We do see him as a storyteller, as are you. You've written two novels. . . .

SA: Two novels, a book of short stories, and seven books of poems.

SBK: But I read when you were growing up, you didn't intend to be a writer at all. You thought you'd be a pediatrician.

SA: Yeah. I was a really sick kid. I was hydrocephalic at birth and had brain surgery. So I spent a lot of time in hospitals, and like most sick kids, I developed this fascination with doctors and white pantyhose. But that's another story! I spent most of my youth working toward [being a doctor], and I got to college and I couldn't handle human anatomy lab. I kept fainting with the cadavers. I had to do something to stay a full-time student, and the only class that fit the schedule was a poetry writing workshop. So fainting and human anatomy led me into writing.

SBK: Where did you go to college?

SA: Washington State University.

SBK: And from whom did you learn poetry?

SA: Alex Kuo.

SBK: So your first poems, when did they start appearing?

SA: That spring, because that first poetry workshop, one of the assignments Alex had was you had to research literary magazines and submit to them. So it was not only the artistic process of learning how to write poems and how to read, but also the professional process of being a writer and trying to get published. I submitted to these little magazines—

Hanging Loose, which eventually published my poetry books; *The Beloit Poetry Journal;* and there was one other one. I sent out three submissions and got three acceptances. It's still what I consider myself.

SBK: You consider yourself a poet first?

SA: I'm a poet who does other things so I can pay the rent.

SBK: So do you still, as you're walking through your day, have poems come to you?

SA: Oh, yeah. I'm always writing down. Everything starts as a poem. Everything.

SBK: Even your short stories?

SA: Yeah. Everything does. Novels start as a poem.

SBK: How do the poems that start off your novels turn into novels or screenplays?

SA: They keep going! [Laughs.] And I just don't have the patience to write an epic poem. So at some point, past a certain page count, a ten-page poem, I'm thinking, "This isn't a poem!" I'm not a big fan of contemporary epic poetry—I'm just not—so as I'm rampaging along in a poem or something, I'm realizing that what this really is is a novel.

SBK: Who were the storytellers for you when you were a kid?

SA: My influences were my dad—he told stories, not traditional stories, Indian stories in that sense, but he just told a lot of stories about growing up, stories about his life. My grandmother, who told traditional stories. And Stephen King, John Steinbeck, and the Brady Bunch.

SBK: So you really had your basic melting pot collection of stories.

SA: Exactly. I work out of two traditions—not only my specific tribal storytelling traditions, but western civ storytelling traditions.

SBK: In the essay you did—I think it was for a book on Discovering Reading—you mention that when you were very young, you all of a sudden had an appreciation for paragraphs. So I'm wondering, now that you've been writing screenplays, do you feel that way about scenes?

SA: You know, the funny thing is . . . I wrote the screenplay and it got shot, and I rewrote during shooting, but it wasn't until I got into the editing room where I started feeling like I knew what scenes were about. It amazes me that screenwriters are not in the editing room more often. It was in the editing room where the producer thought I should become a director, as well.

The vocabulary of shots I had in my head I didn't realize I had until then. It wasn't until the editing room that I realized I could figure out what a scene is. In *Smoke Signals*, the screenplay, I didn't know any of the rules—quote unquote rules—so I violated them constantly.

SBK: Such as?

SA: Monologues. Twenty-seven flashbacks. [Laughs.] Long, long wide shots with characters walking and talking—all sorts of cinematic things I violated. And in most cases, they worked in the movie. But being in the editing room, and working with those scenes that didn't necessarily work and seeing how you could write them better is really helping me a lot, especially in the new screenplay I'm working on. [The new one] is based on my novel, *Indian Killer*, a murder mystery-serial killer thing, where there are police interrogations.

So I'm learning the amount of information you can reveal without anybody actually saying anything. The editing room is where I learned the value of action without dialogue. You know, a screenwriter can have just that same kind of vision of what to see and how to tell the story that way—it's not the sole province of the director.

SBK: What were you watching when you had some of these understandings?

SA: Oh, God. I guess the big moment was there's a scene that's not in the movie now, where Victor and Thomas were leaving Phoenix and Suzy Song. I wrote it as an end to the second act, but watching it, it ended up feeling like it was an end to the movie. Seeing that in the editing room, I realized that scene didn't work because it didn't bridge between the scenes before and after it. So that was one of the big moments for me in the editing room, seeing how, rather than treating each scene as a static moment, each scene has to keep moving. So that's what I learned from that—to keep the movie moving forward.

SBK: In the credits for Smoke Signals, *you give thanks to the Sundance Institute. You went to the Sundance Screenwriters Lab?*

SA: Yeah, with this project, Chris Eyre, the director, went to the directors lab, and I was at the screenwriters lab, so we both went with the project.

SBK: Did you both get accepted for the two different arms of it, or how did that work?

SA: The project itself got accepted, so we went to both. The directors lab is three or four weeks, and the screenwriting lab is for a week after that.

SBK: What did you learn there?

SA: The big thing I learned was about moments—about big moments—beats, to use a phrase. The greatest moment I remember from the Institute was we were having a conference with Kit Carson, and we were talking about the scene at the end on the bridge. It was just a rough scene at that point—I was just brainstorming with the ashes. And at one point, Kit grabbed this pop can off the table like it was the ashes, and literally kneeled down and curled up on the floor, so he got the emotion of the moment, and right at the moment he did that, I saw the ashes blowing past his face in my head.

That physical action of talking about the story with a screenwriter like Kit Carson, when he did that fetal movement—that's when I saw the end of the movie. So those moments are what happen there. Talking about the story, talking about the screenplay enabled me to see ways in which to actually visualize the story.

SBK: I'm trying to get a picture of what the directors lab and the screenwriters lab actually look like when you're there in them—what all goes on.

SA: We shoot scenes from the screenplay, with actors brought in. We have whole crews, etc. They shoot four scenes in the directors lab. And then the screenwriters lab, they have screenwriters coming in and have conferences with the screenwriter to talk about the project.

SBK: And what did you learn that maybe wasn't part of the curriculum?

SA: [Laughs.] That screenwriters wish that they were novelists. That screenwriters, no matter how successful, wish they were successful novelists. It was funny. We had all these incredible screenwriters who were much more interested in my literary career—who had written these incredible movies and were making literally millions of dollars, I'm sure, and they wanted to talk about my little literary books. And my book touring. Reading to twelve people in Des Moines, Iowa.

SBK: Has that happened to you?

SA: Yeah.

SBK: Just twelve?

SA: Well, not any more, but in the beginning. So it was really fascinating to see. I know why now, being in the movie world and seeing how screenwriters get treated. And then seeing how as a novelist, I'm Fidel Castro—I'm the dictator of my world—I'm treated like a king wherever I go. And screenwriters, you're the peons, the untouchables.

SBK: Were you at Sundance when Smoke Signals *got the Audience Award?*

SA: Yeah, I was there the whole time. It's so funny. Nobody really cares that I've had dinner with Norman Mailer and met Toni Morrison or rubbed shoulders with Philip Roth or anything like that, but as soon as they hear that Ally Sheedy gave me a hug, they go crazy. Movies are really this huge American mythic thing. It really is the oral tradition for us. And it brings out all that. . . . There's nothing that binds people together like a movie. It's the most tribal thing for us, as Americans, as world citizens, really.

SBK: Of all the poems, novels, screenplays, you said you feel like a poet. Which is your favorite—poetry, still?

SA: Poetry. Screenplays are really poetry. They're like sonnets. There are certain formal expectations of a screenplay and you have to know those and you have to work with those. You can certainly violate conventions or challenge conventions, but you have to use those conventions in a way or violate those conventions in a way that are thematic. Let's say in a sonnet you're in iambic pentameter the whole time, and you change the meter for a line based on a thematic reason—say you had a line that was a very emotional line, so you wanted to break apart the meter, you would.

In a screenplay that works the same way. For instance, in *Smoke Signals*, it's a basic three-act structure with the structure of a buddy movie, but it stops at certain points for people to tell stories. So when Arnold tells the Jesuit basketball monologue in the middle of the movie, that really is a dramatic pause, a breaking of the structure of the screenplay. It was for thematic reasons.

And screenplays are all about images, as well. Images propel the story, and that's what poetry does. I feel a real kinship between poetry and screenplay writing. I'm much more comfortable writing screenplays, for instance, than I am writing fiction. Poetry is the most natural form for me, but screenplays feel more natural to me than fiction does.

SBK: I'm curious about your experience with novels that is less comfortable.

SA: They're marathons of pain. [Laughs.]

SBK: How so?

SA: Frankly, sometimes I get bored with my characters. Sometimes it ends up feeling like a dinner party you can never leave.

SBK: It's true. You have to stay till the bitter end. Anybody else can pick it up and put it down, but you've got to stay.

SA: Exactly. And all those things about storytelling I'm most interested in are not necessarily novelistic.

SBK: Interesting. Like what?

SA: I read some novels that go on and on about detail about the leaves on a tree and the neighborhood, and I suppose they're trying to be poetic, but they're not. Novels are macro imagery. Poetry is micro imagery. I'm more interested in micro. I could really care less, for instance, what kind of clothes a person is wearing. Or the way a tree in the yard looks.

SBK: That's funny. I put off writing novels for years because I didn't want to describe shrubbery.

SA: But my reviews, the negative reviews I get are because I don't get into that kind of stuff.

SBK: But what kind of reviews do you get about your dialogue and the things that are happening in them?

SA: Oh, that part's great. And I'll keep writing novels because it's a challenging form, and you can do things in a novel you can't do anywhere else.

SBK: Do you pay attention to your reviews?

SA: Oh, of course. Anybody who says they don't is lying. I like well-written reviews, whether they're positive or negative. Most often, the most well-written, incisive reviews are at least in some part negative. And that's what you can learn from.

SBK: Are there some things that you've noted from the reviews of Smoke Signals?

SA: The response has been about 80 percent positive, which is great. And the negative ones so far have really been funny. *Entertainment Weekly,* Owen Gleiberman, in sort of a Sundance roundup, said that the screenplay was Screenplay Manual 101, which just made me laugh. I wrote him a letter. I said, "Okay, Owen, find me the screenplay manual that suggests using twenty-seven flashbacks, nineteen monologues, and Indians."

SBK: One of the things about the movie is that it's very self-confident, and it's also very willing to laugh at itself.

SA: You know, that's how I am. Indians are funny and very self-deprecating in their humor. And that's never been portrayed on screen before. . . . You haven't seen these characters before. Especially Thomas Builds-a-Fire. Nothing remotely approaching him has existed on screen before. He's the trickster. He's Hamlet. He's Candide. He comes from a long line of many traditions of the trickster figure in all sorts of cultures.

SBK: Wearing his "Frybread Power" t-shirt.

SA: He's also the most unreliable narrator of all time.

SBK: That's true. By the end of the movie we think, "He'll tell a story about anything."

SA: Exactly. Whether he knows anything about the thing or not.

SBK: So what is your writing day like?

SA: Well, I'm a recovering alcoholic, and when I drank I was a binge drinker. So really I'm a binge writer. I'll work twelve to fourteen hours a day for weeks at a time, and then I won't write for weeks at a time.

SBK: Twelve to fourteen hours a day—don't you get exhausted?

SA: Nah. There is nothing in the world I would rather do than write.

SBK: I heard that you have a new baby. . . .

SA: That's the only thing that challenges that, ever. This is the only point at which I am going to get an outside office to work in, because it is so easy to hear him upstairs laughing and walk upstairs now. Even my wife is fully aware of the fact that I would rather be writing than spend time with her. We are very independent, but he has really changed us both in that way. . . which is great.

SBK: But so far you've been writing at home?

SA: Yeah.

SBK: And do you write on a computer?

SA: Yeah. I write in Final Draft. I'm a Mac man. Poetry I often write on notebooks. But fiction and screenplays I write on the computer.

SBK: And you must carry a notebook with you all the time, yeah?

SA: Yeah. I'm addicted to stationery. Organizers, notebooks, pens, papers, desk calendars, filing cabinets, file folders. I'm constantly altering the way in which I organize myself. And I'm never actually organized, but organization paraphernalia is always changing around me. I have to organize my organizing material!

SBK: So you're one of those guys who can't walk by an office supply store without stopping in, right?

SA: I will go into stores and not buy anything. I'll often just go up and down and fondle the papers.

SBK: Let me ask you a little more about that literary career. You've won all kinds of awards for your poetry as well as your fiction, including a citation for the Pen/Hemingway Award. What exactly is the Pen/Hemingway Award?

SA: I was runner-up for the Best First Fiction award. It's the Best First Fiction.

SBK: And what kind of difference did that make for you?

SA: All those awards just heighten visibility, essentially. It gets booksellers to pay attention to the books. When it's written on the cover of a book, people read it, so it ends up being like the Good Housekeeping Seal of Approval: "This book is safe." [Laughs.]

SBK: Did you feel any pressure after having won the citation?

SA: Not really. Raymond Carver in a poem talks about gravy. It's all gravy to me. I guess the best way I can put this is from the movie *Broadcast News*, when William Hurt says to Albert Brooks, "What do you do when your reality exceeds your dreams?" You know, I'm a kid from the rez, so getting a book published and being moderately successful was far beyond anything I ever dreamed of, so being very successful is incredible. Walking on the moon for me.

A CONVERSATION WITH . . .

Stephen Schiff

You may have known him first as a film critic for the Boston *Phoenix*, where he was nominated for a Pulitzer. Or as the film critic for *Fresh Air with Terry Gross*. Or as a writer of profiles for *Vanity Fair* or *The New Yorker*.

But when Stephen Schiff was hired to write his first screenplay, he didn't imagine he'd be known as the guy who wrote the screenplay for the movie that, once made, looked as though it might never be seen in the U.S.

Fortunately, however, Showtime decided to take a chance on *Lolita*. And then the Samuel Goldwyn Co. picked it up for theatrical release. So this new rendering of Vladimir Nabokov's novel, which opened for an Academy-qualifying week in L.A. theatres in July, will be shown on Showtime in August. And, finally, in theatres in September. *Lolita, the Book of the Film,* has just been published by Applause Books.

Since writing the screenplay for *Lolita*, Stephen Schiff has been hired to write a host of other screen adaptations of novels, along with a couple of originals. Right before Goldwyn picked up *Lolita*, Stephen Schiff talked from his home in New York about how he first got involved with this project.

<u>STEPHEN SCHIFF:</u> It was around 1990 that the Nabokov estate was auctioning various properties, and among these was *Lolita*. And my friend Lili Zanuck, whom I'd known for years, called up and said, "You know, you'd be the right guy to write *Lolita*." And this gave me pause. Because someone who's been writing in a public, widely read way about movies often gets asked to write screenplays. And I just never could see it. I never thought (*a*) that it would interest me as writing—which was naive of me, but there you go, and (*b*) I thought just because I know movies and just because I can write, doesn't mean I can write movies. Nevertheless, the idea of creating a coherent artistic response to *Lolita*, one of the most beloved books of my reading list, fascinated me, so I began.

And what I did was I very naively wrote all dialogue, which tells you that I knew nothing about writing a screenplay. Not that I didn't know that there were supposed to be stage directions, or rather screen directions, but that I didn't have the patience to write them, so I would just write "stage directions to come"— "TK" in journalese.

What I later discovered, as I became a screenwriter, was that you see the entire movie in your mind, and the distinction between dialogue and screen directions is a false one; that it just, as you're writing, tumbles out all of a piece. At least, that's my experience.

I wrote 30 to 40 pages, and then Lili called back and said, rather presciently, "Why don't you forget about it. In this political atmosphere, this movie could never be made, anyway. Sorry I led you astray."

So I said, 'Well, that's that," and I went on with my life.

SBK: Had Lili known that you were a Nabokov fan?

<u>SS:</u> No, I actually think she had not. I think she thought of me, rightly or wrongly, as sort of a literary person. And she was my dear, dear friend, and she was always trying to entice me into screenwriting or something else. But she hit a chord with this idea.

SBK: When did envisioning a whole film—images as well as dialogue—fall into place for you?

<u>SS:</u> The moment I began writing *Lolita* the second time. I completely threw out my first version and never referred to it again.

SBK: So you didn't begin the first version with the beginning words from the novel, as you did the final version?

SS: Actually I don't remember that. I was just writing scenes and thinking how a beginning might be. I think I started in a mental hospital, because that's sort of where Humbert Humbert is writing from. But I threw it away and began again. Also, the second time I began writing, I had met with Adrian [Lyne] and Richard Zanuck, and there was a feeling of what we were interested in doing together, if indeed we moved on together, which eventually we did.

SBK: I read you had conversations with Adrian Lyne for about a month before you began writing. . . .

SS: No, that's not quite true. He and I had a couple of conversations—one before the first draft was written, and then another one during the writing of the first draft. We didn't get down to the development process as it usually exists until after I had written my first draft and he had decided to make a movie from it. But Adrian had gone through the book and developed an outline. . . .

SBK: What did that outline consist of?

SS: It consisted of pages—a page number and a one-line description of what was happening. For instance, I'm looking at page 3. At the top it says, "Page 29—Humbert's break-up with his former wife—could be funny as a flashback, maybe," and then he copies down the passage from the book. "Page 34—Humbert talks about his bout with insanity." "Page 36—Humbert's arrival at the Hayes house, greeted by the yapping dog." It's notes of the things that he liked, and when you're working closely with a director whose dream project it is, and who's read the book five hundred times, it's nice to have that outline, and you pick and choose.

I love working with a good director, because I have sometimes thought that if you're just hired to do an idea by a studio or producer, it's like being the world's greatest dart player. You're coming into this contest where you have to show everyone how great you are at playing darts. And you discover when you enter the room that the dart board could be anywhere.

Whereas, working with a director, it's there in front of you and you know where to aim.

SBK: Here you were tackling a book with precious little dialogue in it. I want to know about beginning a script where you had to create the dialogue. And it's dialogue of Nabokov's book, which is so highly revered.

SS: Well, there are a number of questions there. One is, "Were you daunted by this masterpiece?" And I plead naiveté. To me, it was just the most welcome of adventures. Of course, I didn't know all the strange things that would happen to the film once it was made. But the confrontation with one of the great masterpieces of the century—to my mind, the greatest novel of the post-War era—why was I not daunted, I have no idea. I felt I could see what would work and what wouldn't work, and what to keep and what to get rid of. And what in Nabokov was exquisite but unfilmable. And what could be written—what I could sort of make up out of thin air that would seem Nabokovian. Many people who have written about the film seem to think that I took vast passages directly from the book. That couldn't be farther from the truth, but I'm somewhat pleased that the illusion is so convincing.

SBK: As you were writing, how aware were you of the censor outside the door?

SS: Meaning the government kind of censor?

SBK: Not necessarily the government censor, but how big for you loomed the question of "Will we or will we not be able to show this on screen—this particular scene, this particular act, this hand on this thigh?"

SS: It didn't loom at all. I mean, not because I was such a babe in the woods. I knew that what we were working on would be controversial. I also knew that everything I was writing was within the strictures of the law. The law has been recently interpreted in ways that are broad enough to allow everything that I was writing, and that was fine. But it was not really part of my process, because—maybe this is the naive part—I was working from an acknowledged masterpiece.

I also knew that self-censorship of any sort is anathema to creation. There's censorship of all kinds when you're writing. And when you're writing professionally for many years, as I have, there are all sorts of turns of mind you could follow that would lead you right to a block if you didn't know better. Some of them are, "Oh, no, this is no good." Some of them are, "Oh, no, they won't like this out there." Some of them are, "Oh, no, they will put me in jail for this."

Those are directions that are not fruitful while you are writing. So the censor at the door, if he or she existed, I didn't know it.

SBK: In this movie, you seem to have a good sense of scene. I know you're no novice to movies. You've been watching movies intently and reviewing them since you were at the Boston Phoenix, *right?*

SS: Yeah. That would be twenty-one years. 1977.

SBK: So were you aware when you were writing of the basic structure of a scene or was that something that just came automatically to you?

SS: I think people would assume, as I would, that I had been thinking along these lines for all these years that I had been watching movies. But no, I hadn't, because (*a*) I had not had any interest in screenwriting or in making movies, and (*b*) I think that unless you do, a critic looks at a movie from a very different standpoint. It's the rare critic who thinks as he's watching a scene in terms of its structure as a scene and what makes a scene work, and all that stuff that we all think of every day when we're writing movies.

And it's very interesting to look back upon my years as a writer of [feature articles] and as a critic and to see just how little I knew and how wrong I was about so many things. And I would defend to the death the critic's right to look up at the screen and see something there that can be judged aesthetically independent of any knowledge of its making.

At the same time, critics so often—and I did, too—impute one or another moments to one or another creators of the film. You know, they have their head filled up with the auteur theory—I had no idea what bunk it is. I just read a review in *The New Yorker* by my friend and wonderful writer Anthony Lane, in which he was talking about how the screenwriter had been very clever to take something that happens on page 70 of the book and put it at the beginning of the film. And I thought to myself, "Well, I just bet he didn't." Maybe he did—it's a wonderful film, wonderful screenwriter—but I'll just bet he didn't. I'll bet the director did that and I'll bet it was in the editing room that it happened and it solved a problem that they had. And all that sort of stuff that actually happens because films don't have authors; films have many authors. And putting that word "author" in the vicinity of film is really to falsify the process.

So all those years of looking at films only partially prepared me. Prepared me only in that they exposed me to film on a broad basis. Now I look at films in such a different way.

In retrospect, the journalistic experiences that prepared me more for screenwriting were writing feature stories—most frequently, cultural profiles. Because a cultural profile is something where you don't have any kind of narrative and you have to create the sensation of narrative momentum out of nothing. It's not like a news story where something happened and then something happened and then something happened.

And you're even working with dialogue. Even though you're not making it up, you're shaping it and winnowing it and trying to make it fun. Trying to make it move, trying to make it tell a story. So that gave me a sense of what a story was and what scenes were, what a setting was, how characters might work—in ways that reviewing movies never did.

SBK: So what was the trickiest part for you in writing this screenplay?

SS: Well, there were lots of artistic challenges. I don't want to portray them as painful or tricky or anything like that. There were interesting questions. For instance, one we've already touched on, which is trying to create an approximation of what seems to many people to be the salient feature of this book, which is style.

You can't actually put the style on the screen. For one thing, there isn't much dialogue, but a screenplay works with dialogue, so you have to convey through made-up dialogue this atmosphere, and you can use a few voice-overs, but too much voice-over is going to wreck the movie.

And besides, the floridity and prolixity of Nabokov's prose is not going to adapt itself as well to voice-over as people may think—it just doesn't work that way. Many of these things are not sayable by an actor in a way that would be anything but ludicrous. So that, of course, was one of the hard parts.

SBK: Very different to read it on the page than to hear it on the screen.

SS: Yeah, very, very different. Secondly, of course, you are dealing with an unreliable narrator, and you are seeing the world through the veil of his obsession. And movies are made of surfaces, so you have to go from the world of internality to the world of externality that movies present without sacrificing a feeling of his psychology and his obsession. But in the book, Lolita is virtually a figment of his imagination, or, as she would say, a fragment of his imagination. And you have to create this flesh-and-blood creature on the screen who is a little like the creature he imagines her to be, but in many ways is not. And since the novel doesn't present that except in glimpses, I had to extrapolate from there.

And finally there's the Quilty character. I mean, this is a book that cannot be understood on one reading by anybody, no matter how smart you are. Because the way Quilty is woven through it is a puzzle, and you don't know what the question is until you get to the end. So how do you make a movie that can be understood on one viewing, and still try to render the Quilty character in a way that was Nabokovian, as opposed to Kubrickian? Kubrick just sort of throws up his hands and says, "We're going to show you this guy every second, and we're going to start with his murder so you never have any doubt about who he is and what it's about." And I think Kubrick's movie should have been called "Quilty." It's about Quilty, and Quilty is the most vivid and marvelous character in it. And Peter Sellers' improvisations are inspired. But it's just very different from what Nabokov was attempting, and I wanted to see if we could do something along those lines, even though it was very challenging.

SBK: Why did you choose to make Lolita fourteen, rather than twelve, as she is in the book?

SS: That was a matter of casting. At the same time, I think that . . . the idea was to have her be a child one second and a woman the next, which is what many teenagers are, and what I think Lolita of the book is. But to actually cast a twelve-year-old would have made the film less accessible and more grotesque in many ways.

I think a lot of people wish we had done that, a lot of pure Nabokovians, but I think we achieved the same effect through better means. Because if the audience could look at this man and this girl and see it as an icky story of child abuse, and not have remotely any idea of what the sexual attraction he felt for her would be or would feel like, then I don't think we've done the job that Nabokov does, and perhaps that the material demands, of putting us inside this completely demented person and feeling his feelings. If you can just sit there in the audience and say, "Ooh, what a creep. That would never be something I would feel or I would understand" . . . I don't think that's a movie worth making or watching.

SBK: After the movie was written and made, was there an interim step of the movie being edited by lawyers?

SS: Well, it wasn't edited by lawyers, but we did have the unfortunate circumstance of having a lawyer in the editing room. In September of 1996, after the film had been shot, but while it was being edited, Orin Hatch, a senator from Utah, got a rider attached to a spending bill which became the Childhood Pornography Prevention Act of 1996. This vaguely worded, probably unconstitutional rider, was directed against people who were on the Internet and were attaching children's heads to adult bodies by computer and selling them or doing whatever. But it was so vaguely worded and so broad that what it was basically saying was you could not seem to portray a child in sexually explicit conduct.

And that "seemed to"—that may not be the exact words, but something very close to it—suddenly threw everything into question, because it meant that even if you had a body double, that could still seem to be a child. I mean, strictly interpreted, the law could be applied to great works of art in museums. So this law came to someone's attention, maybe Adrian's, and everyone just panicked. Visions of being hauled off to jail— the mandatory penalties on the law are very high. And of course *Lolita* was thought by many people to be a very obvious target if someone wanted either, for their own aggrandizement, to use the law, or test the law.

Batteries of lawyers were hired, and the least Draconian of those lawyers was invited into the editing room by the owners of the film. And very, very important scenes in the film were going to be removed.

I talked to a lawyer named Edward de Grazia, who had written this wonderful book called *Girls Lean Back Everywhere: the Law of Obscenity and the Assault on Genius,* which is a history of obscenity law.

Ed was this guy who had, according to the liner notes of the book, been responsible for freeing from censorship Aristophanes' *Lysistrata,* Henry Miller's *Tropic of Cancer,* William Burroughs' *Naked Lunch,* and the Swedish film, *I am Curious, Yellow.* So I called him to have him arm me with law, and we went to work.

There were two scenes in particular that [the lawyer in the editing room] wanted out of the film, and they were crucial, wonderful scenes. One of them was the scene in which she's reading the comics, and the lawyer was saying "There's no way you can edit that scene that will make it allowable." He was going way, way over the top. He was not only interpreting the law, but he was anticipating new laws that didn't exist, and it just shouldn't happen to a dog that you have a lawyer in the editing room, and if you did, only dogs would be directors.

SBK: But that scene remained.

SS: That scene remained because of a moment that was sort of thrilling to me. We were getting down to brass tacks. A lot of nudity was cut out, not because it had to be by law, but because everyone was so scared, and we had to listen to this guy, supposedly.

So we had to cut out things. But at a certain point, Adrian was playing good cop, and I was playing bad cop. And the lawyer was being obdurate. Finally the comics scene was about to bite the dust, and Adrian and I reversed roles. He just went into a tirade that was beautiful and terrifying to see. And it created a very nice mood in a way that the lawyer was petrified. But I knew he would not be swayed by it. And then I said to him, "Let me ask you something. What does the statute say?"

And the lawyer said, "It says that we cannot only not have any depiction of a child having explicit sex; we can't even have the appearance of a child having explicit sex."

So I said, "What's the wording?"

And he said, "The act outlaws 'any visual depiction where such visual depiction is or appears to be of a minor engaging in sexually explicit conduct.'"

And that "appears to be" is the point. I said, "Well, wait . . . with all due respect, I have to tell you that you've misunderstood the statute."

He said, "Huh?"

I said, "The law says nothing about what appears or doesn't appear to be explicit sex. The definition of sexually explicit conduct has not changed, and there is plenty of legal precedent that has established that.

The words 'appears to be' don't refer to the sex, they refer to the child. So if there appears to be a child engaged in sexually explicit conduct, we're in trouble, but since there's no sexually explicit conduct anywhere in this movie, we're fine."

There was this long silence, and the lawyer said, "Let me look at the scene again." And we ran it again, and this time he said, "You know, I'm seeing what the changes you've made do. I missed that little cut there, and you know, I think you've got something here. No, I can live with this. This is going to be fine."

SBK: Just how crazy has it made you that Lolita*'s met with such problems in distribution?*

SS: You know, this is my first movie, and everything about it has been so peculiar. I mean, nothing like this has ever happened in the history of film.

SBK: In terms of . . . ?

SS: In terms of what happened to this major, big-budget adaptation of an acknowledged classic novel by one of the most successful directors working today being de facto banned. So I've been watching it half in frustration and half in open-mouthed wonder, because what's going to happen next? How could people say to Adrian Lyne that it was his best film and mean it, which I think some of them did, because they said it to other people who were in their confidence and not in Adrian's confidence, and then just absolutely say "No way are we going to distribute it"?

You know, it was a very tricky moment politically. It was certainly bad timing that this film came to completion at the moment of the Jon-Benet Ramsey murder and at the moment of the Belgian sex crimes and at the moment of this kind of rising hysteria. And one had seen parallels to this in the way movies were being generally blamed for all sorts of ills, from the loss of manners and civility among young people to violence in the streets, even as the crime rate was plummeting in major cities like New York.

All this was in the air and I kept thinking to myself, "What do people really think? Do they think that someone will go into a movie theatre, watch this movie, and say, 'Hey, pedophilia! Great idea! Think I'll try it!'?" Are they so unsophisticated as to believe that just to depict something on the screen is to endorse it? We do live in a moment when people are extremely uncomprehending about the uses of art, if film can be dignified with that term.

I grew up in an age where the culture was expanding, in which new things could be explored. And it was good. Now suddenly to watch the culture contracting, and people getting afraid of culture and of expression and of art and people wanting to understand less. . . . This process that is at the center of narrative art, of entering the world or the mind of someone completely other than you, and someone whose actions you would never condone but in fact would condemn, but understanding that person—the idea that that would be wrong and frightening and shameful had always been on the fringes of our culture, but now to see it coming into prominence again was shocking and dismaying.

And then to wonder is it really true, or is it just that the gatekeepers of the culture think it's true?

We've forgotten that one of the roles of . . . I keep using this word "art"—I'm sorry, I should apologize for it . . . but one of the roles of art or would-be art or maybe culture is to make us feel uncomfortable. I wouldn't make that a test for something, whether it made you feel uncomfortable or not as whether it's art or not, but it's one of its functions.

SBK: And if it's going to be any kind of mirror at all, there are parts of the murky ooze that are going to be reflected.

SS: Have to be. Otherwise, what is it? Otherwise it's just dumb spectacle. And dumb spectacle's plenty of fun, but a diet of circuses is insufficient.

1998

A CONVERSATION WITH . . .

Neil LaBute

Neil LaBute is not a flincher. He didn't flinch with *In The Company of Men*, when putting his characters' less-than-noble thoughts on screen, and he doesn't flinch in his latest, *Your Friends and Neighbors*, when zooming into what might otherwise have been their most intimate moments.

Initially a playwright and drama professor, Neil was graduated from Brigham Young University, the University of Kansas, and New York University, and received a fellowship to London's Royal Court Theatre. It was one of his plays that caught the attention of film producers, and it was while waiting to get that project financed that Neil took another of his scripts and got his first movie made, as he says, "sort of by default."

That first movie, *In the Company of Men*, won the Independent Spirit Award for Best Screenplay, the 1997 Filmmakers Trophy at Sundance, and was designated Best First Feature by the New York Film Critics Circle.

Married for fifteen years, Neil lives with his family in Fort Wayne, Indiana. Shortly before *Your Friends and Neighbors* was to open, he sat in the Hotel Nikko and talked about the beginnings of the film, which I had heard began life as a play.

<u>Neil LaBute:</u> That's actually sort of a myth. It started as a screenplay, but the first time I got a chance to put it on its feet was through a theatre company. So I made some changes that were necessitated by its being on stage, but it began life as something I saw for the screen.

SBK: How long ago?

<u>NL:</u> A couple years now. Not too long.

SBK: Do you remember the movie It Could Happen to You? *It was originally called* Cop Gives Waitress $2 Million Tip, *with Nic Cage, Bridget Fonda?*

<u>NL:</u> Oh, sure.

SBK: That began from Jane Anderson saying, "I'd like to do something about generosity."

<u>NL:</u> Really?

SBK: Uh-huh. She was playing with the notion of generosity as she was beginning to write that. So did you have the same kind of thoughts as you were . . .

<u>NL:</u> Yeah. Generosity. That's what I was thinking. [Laughs.] I didn't get much of it in, did I?

SBK: [Laughs.]

<u>NL:</u> You know, I don't remember what it is exactly that sparked this. With *In the Company of Men,* I can remember specifically. It was the line "Let's hurt somebody." It was that calculated idea of "Let's go out of our way to do damage to someone."

But this was much more mathematical, in a way. I set a series of parameters by saying, "I'm going to do something where the characters won't speak the other person's names, it'll all be interior, it'll only be those six people talking. So this is the theorem, and now let's see where it takes us."

And I know that this infidelity will set off a chain reaction amongst them. But it's logical to me; it's sort of mathematical. Often I find myself writing and it's precise without being calculated. I'm not one who ends up putting Post-its all over the house that you could follow the trail and say "This is where I started, and I know what each of these scenes is going to be." I like the idea of plunging off into the dark, saying it should be as interesting to write as it is to watch.

And I do write myself into corners. I'll go "Hmmmm" five scenes into this, "This isn't making sense," and I'll have to backpedal or throw something out. But I like the idea that I know these characters will all meet, but I don't know how I'm actually going to make Amy's character meet Jason's character—will they meet in passing? And then I came to the point of view that, oh, no, they're going to end up together. It seems on the surface almost illogical, and yet it makes perfect sense in the math side of it that those are the two characters who haven't met yet, and in the sense that here's a woman who's searching, and she fails relatively miserably with the different kinds of men who are in the script, so why wouldn't she end up with this guy who has a very close relationship with her ex-husband?

So upon reflection, you go, "Oh, that actually makes pretty good sense," you know? I like that sense of discovery for myself—it keeps it interesting that somewhere down the line, you know something has to happen, but you don't force it, really. You go, "Okay, I'll write until it makes sense." And a lot of that has to do with rewriting, which I used to be scared of.

At first I was writing plays, but I was only writing one-act plays when I started, because I almost froze, like in terror, at the thought of stopping. How can people be in the middle of writing this world that they're creating on their paper or on their computer, and then stop and close it and go watch television and eat dinner and go to bed and come back to it the next day? I used to write in binges.

SBK: So you'd write that whole one-act at one time.

NL: Yeah. It was sort of like alcoholic. It was like, "I'm starting now, and I will not stop until I'm done." So you end up with a lot of little one-act plays which are hard to get produced in this country! It was a barrier that I had put in front of myself, that I hated the idea of stopping. I've gotten over it now by just doing it, by saying, "See, you can stop and you can go back to it." It was just one of those personal quirks that everybody has. I never had writer's block, but I had writer's fear of stopping.

SBK: Where did you have your plays produced?

NL: Chicago, L.A., New York, and I did some in London, but all the time teaching. . . . And sort of by default, in a way, I ended up doing a first film.

SBK: By default?

NL: Well, by someone seeing a play and asking if I would make it into a screenplay, and then by making that screenplay, being introduced to the world of independent film financing, which is the most labyrinth-like thing, of how people get these little bits of money together to make pictures. And because of having done theatre, where I'd always liked environmental stuff that never really cost a great deal. You were finding plays to fit spaces, like you found a great basement. . . . "Okay, what play do we know that we could do in this basement? This would be great for *The Dumbwaiter,* because it's a dank basement. We'll put the audience down here."

Because of that, it was never a huge financial concern. And then suddenly when you find out just at the most base level, there's real expense behind making a movie . . . beyond all the deferments you can make and all of that, there are still certain things that people just don't give you unless you have the money, like getting film and lab time. So once I started dealing with this other group who were trying to raise the money to make a film, it just seemed to go on and on, and I thought, "My God, I don't know how people make movies!" It was like you spent a year of your life just trying to raise money.

At that point I got frustrated, and I had also seen enough examples of people like Kevin Smith and Robert Townsend who were making films on a regional basis—taking a little bit of money and utilizing what they had available for free and making these pictures. Robert Rodriguez, Ed Burns . . . Rose Troche and Guinevere Turner, the women who did *Go Fish* . . . every year at Sundance you hear these tales. Of course, a lot of them are romanticized, because you hear one figure, but by the time we see it on the screen, more money has been poured into it. But it sounds great to say, "It cost me twenty-five grand," which, like *In the Company of Men,* we did shoot for that much money. . . .

SBK: Twenty-five grand?

NL: Yeah, twenty-five grand we shot it for, but there were a lot of defer-ments at that point, and by the time you see it on the screen it's probably a quarter of a million. That's still not a lot, but it's a lot more than $25,000. But had I known that amount at that point, I probably would-n't have done it. I had just heard the figures that make good copy in the paper, and you're like, "Well, I can get that much money." So that's what I did, and that's what we shot it for.

SBK: So you jumped both feet into the labyrinth of finding money?

NL: Yeah, I got two friends to put in $10,000 each, because they'd been in a car accident and I knew they had a settlement. They were fine, but they each had ten grand, and I was like, "Will you gamble on this?" And they were like, "Yeah, let's take a shot." And then one of our actors put money in, and we were off.

SBK: When you were originally approached to turn In the Company of Men *into a movie . . .*

NL: Oh, I'm sorry. It wasn't that play. It wasn't *In the Company of Men.* It was a play called *Rounder.* It was a play that had been at the Sundance Playwrights Festival. I only did *In the Company of Men* because that was a script I felt I could do for that amount of money. It wasn't the same piece.

SBK: Oh. Somebody approached you about doing Rounder . . .

NL: And waiting for that to be financed, I finally said, "I'm going to do *In the Company of Men* myself." Because *In the Company of Men* just had the three main characters, and it was a very concentrated scenario that I felt I could make look good and come off as a film for that amount of money.

SBK: So that's what you mean when you say you kind of sidled into it. You were trying to get another movie made.

NL: Yeah. And which I would only have been the writer for. But it was just that unbelievable wait.

SBK: Getting back to Your Friends and Neighbors, *you have succeeded once again in plumbing new depths in the meanness of men, in the Jason Patric character.*

NL: Well, thank you.

SBK: I should tell you up front that I don't know how anybody can imagine that you're misogynistic if they've actually seen what you've done with these guys.

NL: I get it over and over.

SBK: And I don't understand that.

NL: Well, it's either taking something at face value or taking the time to read between the lines a bit. And it's either overtly what's said or. . . .

SBK: This guy is not a hero.

NL: He's sure not.

SBK: Neither were the guys in In the Company of Men.

NL: Right. And Jason's character even is very quick to say that he doesn't see himself as that. He sees himself as this is his life, and he's not going to let anybody get in the way of him enjoying it. He's very straightforward and he's very honest—frighteningly honest. You wish he would lie. It's like, "Do me a favor—I don't want to hear the truth."

The only thing that's funny in there to me is that these friends would ever, after hearing one or two of those stories, refer to him in terms of "What do you think? " because he says the most audacious things. Yet Barry, sort of living vicariously, continually is like, "What's your best?" And then it's like, "Oh, my God, I'm sorry I asked!"

And yet he has qualities . . . He sticks up for his friends. He's one of the only people in the movie that says "I'm sorry." He's honest—again to a fault, he's so aggressively honest—but he is at least honest. Everybody else tends to lie or hide the truth. Even somebody I care about, like Amy's character, when given the chance to say, "I'm sorry about what I did," she just stares at [the Aaron Eckhart character]. "What do you want me to say?" she says. And he says, "Nothing, I guess." They just cannot communicate, these people. The second they bring it up, she's moving out. They cannot face the truth.

That's what I like about those kinds of characters—even the ones like Jason, who are very aggressive, or Aaron, who's so pathetic in many ways—they have their up and down days, like everybody else. Some days I'm at my best, and other days I make the bad choices and I'm not as funny or as nice as I can be. What I like about them is that no one is singled out as the bad guy and the good guy. To me, for my money, Ben's character is probably more despicable than Jason's character, because he professes to be of a higher morality. You know, he's better than Jason. And yet he's so awful.

SBK: That's an interesting take on it. I was thinking as I was watching that it seems the women are the only ones who know what they want. The characters here have such a difficult time asking for what they want, or even figuring out what they want.

NL: Absolutely. At least the women, if they don't know what they want, they're honestly searching. Amy doesn't seem to know exactly what it is; she does say "I just want to be held," but it doesn't happen in the way she imagines it. Catherine's character is someone I really like. She's the assertive side of Jason's aggression. She doesn't mince words, but she's just a good solid realist who I think wants better than she ends up getting. She ends up with sort of the same person she started out with. But I like her candidness. It's kind of nice to write a character that has at their disposal the lines that you always want. She can be pretty caustic, but she does have a refreshing candor.

SBK: This movie is so focused and tight. When you were writing it, how long did it take you in that first stretch?

NL: One long night.

SBK: Was it?

NL: That's how I see it! No. It tends to come pretty fast, the physical writing, but I tend to mull things over a lot. I tend to walk around, bumping into things, going, "What if so-and-so did . . . ," trying to work it out in my head because it's pretty petrifying to look at the screen or look at paper. So physically writing, it was a matter of a couple weeks, probably. Not too long. But the mulling over process, I couldn't even say.

SBK: As you were getting ready to write, what were some of the ideas you were wrestling with at that time, or grappling with, or just wanting to bounce about?

NL: Well, betrayal, always. It's such a fascinating topic to me, that intimate betrayal of tight-knit groups of people who begin to turn on one another—I've always been fond of that. But something like communication . . . It's gone from being a "me" generation to a "me-me-me" generation, where people are so bloodthirsty about getting their needs met that there's no halfway point—it's literally every person for themselves. They almost aren't even aware that other people have needs, because they're so feral about getting what they want.

So that idea was interesting to me, to take a group of people who are talking about a similar topic, which is sexuality, and have that theme run through of "what's your best?" And the women can't quite place it— they're not sure that they've had it yet—and the men either have some sort of absurd cliché notion of "Oh, I'm married, so it's my wife," or "Quite honestly, it's me—when I'm by myself, it never feels better than that." Or down to Jason's character sort of pathologically telling the story that I really believe that he believes. Whether it's true or not, he is quite certain that that rape was the best and most communal experience he ever had.

And Jason was very committed to that, everything from . . . the first lines of the film, you can hear him in the dark talking about, "You want me to turn you over?" And every woman he talks about in the movie is "She's face down. I turn her over by her hair." It's always somebody that faces away from him and simulating that experience, down to the way that [Jason's character] would not look people in the eye. You don't know if he's ashamed of what he is or if he doesn't like other people, he thinks that he's better or he doesn't trust them. . . .

He really isolated some nice character things that created that whole sense of isolation that we tried in everything from doing a film that's inside, yet shooting it super 35, so we have these huge interiors and putting the faces over in the corner of the frame. Or using those Alex Katz pictures for the titles . . . the sense of being alone in a crowded room. We sort of went with the idea of it being like a quarantine: there's the world out there, but these people aren't allowed to go out and mingle because their moral leprosy will rub off on everybody else.

SBK: And then there's Jason poking the eyes out of the fetus.

NL: Yeah, and playing with it, and then at the end he's the proud poppa-to-be, "A few months from now . . ." All that kind of stuff is fun to play with—saying, "What keeps an audience off guard or thinking?"

SBK: You and Kevin Smith and Atom Egoyan all do something—you seem sort of unbridled with your characters. They say things that we're not used to hearing on screen. And yet, they're very human thoughts. As you're writing, do you ever look back and say, "Have I gone over the edge here?"

NL: You know, I try not to, because if you start to censor yourself, then there's not much hope that you're going to say anything that's true. Often the thing that you think is so removed from any kind of controversy still manages to offend someone. It's just an unwinnable equation that I am going to please everyone. So you really have to step away from it and rely on the fact that you're not a mutant and that you're the only person out there who would ever like this . . . that there must be a group of you somewhere. And, I think, get to a healthy place where it's not contingent on "If I get more positive reviews than negative, then it was good. If it made money, it was good." You can get into such a game of qualifying success, you know. I think more people in this country should live by those kind of European maxims—it's not "you're as good as your last work," but "you're as good as your best." I love that whole idea of if you did one book, and that's all you ever did, that was one more than most other people do.

SBK: I want to ask you about that wonderful repetition of scene with the Nastassja Kinski character, looking at the fourth wall, and how that came about.

NL: I love the idea of the repetition of using the same shot and the same dialogue, but people having different wants and the scene always veering off in some different direction. And being able to see her progression at work from being as interested as she is in Catherine to, by the time she's met Ben, she's tired with this picture, she's tired with these men.

Also it was a nice way to show a simple difference of the way men and women can look at the same thing and see something completely different. Because the men always seem to be looking at the picture slightly askew, and the women are always looking at it straight on. And you don't know what they're looking at. At the end of Jason's piece with Nastassja, he's sort of looking at the painting, and then he turns his head. And then Aaron's character is saying, "Isn't it sort of out of whack?" And Ben's character is like, "Your painting's crooked." The men are always seeing it slightly off, and the women have no problem with it. And Nastassja sort of refreshingly says, "No, I think it's you."

That becomes like the brutal phrase in the movie. It sounds like one of those caring, Phil Donahue, "Is it me?" but they never mean it. Barry by the end is alone. If you don't realize it's you, you're in trouble. You can't even get yourself off any more, and you still wonder if it's you. And Jason is quite sure it's not him. "Is it me? No, I don't think so." And Ben is already onto another phrase, practically, before he gets out. So it becomes this sort of blackjack the men use to sound like they care what women think but yet could care less. But Nastassja's the one who says, "No, I think it's you."

It also helps show how in control she is in the workplace and yet is as needy as everybody else, because she's this object of desire but ultimately just somebody who wants to be held and told that they're lovely. So that repetition I found attractive in that way.

SBK: What's the most important thing you learned from playwriting that helps the screenwriting?

NL: For me, it's probably not to be afraid of language. I think language goes in and out of fashion in movies. And I have such a respect for it. When I, with *In the Company of Men*, got a review and had someone like Roger Ebert say, "In this film, words are action," or Janet Maslin saying something like—because I wanted that film to be in black and white, so I controlled the color, but it is in color—to hear her at the end of her review say, "The film's ideas are so stark that it almost seems like it was in black and white," you realize the power of the word.

When we got an NC-17 for this movie the first go-around, at first I was shocked. "For what? What's in it? These people are talking. There's no nudity. There's no violence. There's nothing." But after that I kind of said,

"Actually I should be a little happy, because it shows that the word still is the most powerful thing out there." There's nothing quite as horrific as Jason sitting and talking about how great this experience was. Had I shown a flashback, it would have been the worst choice I could have ever made, to put it in tangible terms. But the juxtaposition of words can make an audience scream or laugh or both at the same time . . . you know, I think I have learned about the power of language, and that's the thing I still respect most. And that's the thing I'm slave to, even making movies, not to the camera.

A CONVERSATION WITH . . .

Tim Cahill
and Stephen Judson

In May 1996, several teams of climbers attempted to scale Mt. Everest. Among them was a team of climbers and filmmakers from Laguna Beach–based MacGillivray Freeman Films, there to film the first ever IMAX movie of Everest.

On May 10, a violent storm came up, threatening the lives of climbers and eventually claiming the lives of eight. The MacGillivray Freeman team put down their cameras and went to help in the rescue effort. Much of this was chronicled in *Into Thin Air*, a book by Jon Krakauer, a climber and writer for *Outside* magazine.

Tim Cahill, Krakauer's colleague at *Outside*, and Steve Judson, director-editor-producer-writer at MacGillivray Freeman, cowrote *Everest*, which was released in March 1998. By August, *Everest* had become the first IMAX film to make *Variety*'s Top 10 Box Office, and was setting records for per-screen averages.

Steve Judson finished Yale as an English major, then went through USC film school as a director-editor, and went to work for Universal. Along the way he worked for Roger Corman—editing, yes, *Student Nurses* and *The Velvet Vampire* before joining Greg MacGillivray, who'd already made a name for himself in the large-format field with *To Fly* and other films.

Tim Cahill's the author of *Pass the Butterworms, Jaguars Ripped My Flesh, A Wolverine Is Eating My Leg,* and a monthly column for *Outside.* Not your stodgy sort of travel writer.

On a day in early July, Steve had just gotten back from a trip to the Bahamas to work on his next movie, about dolphins. He talked for a while, and then called Tim at his home in Livingston, Montana, so Tim could join in the conversation by speakerphone. Before Tim came aboard, though, Steve talked about the differences between editing an IMAX film and a 35mm feature:

STEVE JUDSON: IMAX films are kind of a hybrid in some ways between feature films and documentaries. They're not really pure form documentaries, so it takes a little time just to get a handle on that. A feature film you have all that coverage and stuff, and you're trying to maximize performance, and you've got close-ups to work with and what not. In an IMAX film, it's very different. You usually try to find your best shots, and give people a sense of environment, a sense of place, and you build sequences around those shots, using very little coverage. It's an entirely different approach that way.

In a regular documentary, you have tons and tons of footage, and you're trying to find the little grains of the moments between people. In an IMAX film, it's much more visually driven, so we're trying to find the key visual moments and then introduce the characters more through voice-over and stuff.

We have to pace our films differently. We find that if we edit the films at too fast a clip, people feel a little cheated because they go to the theatre in order to soak in these images, and if you don't leave them up on the screen very long, they feel that they're missing something.

SBK: It is really true. You sit there, like in The Living Sea, *and you want to part through the kelp as you're sitting there.*

SJ: That was the most fun film just from a pure editorial standpoint. It was a film that we restructured very, very much in the editing room. And incidentally, that's the first time that Tim Cahill and I really worked closely together.

SBK: So how much of the actual "doing" do you do? In other words, were you down there in the kelp beds for The Living Sea *when it was shot?*

SJ: Not at all. What I do varies from movie to movie. There are many movies where I never leave Laguna Beach. And there are other movies where I'm there for every frame of the production.

SBK: Who all went on the Everest climb?

SJ: Basically there were four filmmakers. There was David Breashears and Robert Schauer—they were the two that went to the summit of Everest. And then there was Brad Olin and myself—neither of us climbers, but we have over thirty years of IMAX experience between the two of us. David and Robert had no IMAX experience. So Brad and I went up as high as Base Camp. It was always planned that we wouldn't go any higher than that, and I was glad about that when I saw how difficult the Khumbu ice fall was. The intent was that we would try to pass along everything that we'd learned about IMAX to David and Robert in the course of making the film up through Base Camp, and from there on, David and Robert would be on their own.

In making the transition from other formats to IMAX, there are certain kind of principles that are very easy to learn, and David Breashears was very quick at picking up on those. There were other differences between IMAX and documentaries and features that are much subtler and harder to learn, and harder even to say what they are, and that's what I was trying to help David with. People come across differently on IMAX film than they do on other film formats. So how you use people within the frame is different in IMAX.

SBK: Can you give me an example of that?

SJ: A simple example would be that we have to make our films for both a flat screen and a dome. And if you have somebody walk in from the side of the frame, as you normally would, on a dome you're going to have a bending, banana-shaped person who's eight stories high. So what do you do with people? How do you move them around? Well, you just have to learn other ways of having people enter frame or exit frame or not have them do it so much, which is frequently what we do in IMAX. But the way you block people, you're more restricted in IMAX. So what you want to do is get beyond that, so you can work with those restrictions and not make the audience feel that the people on screen are restricted and nailed in place. And that takes a little rethinking.

Other things are just the way performances have to be shaded differently for IMAX. Something that seems fine in 35mm may feel over the top in IMAX. In the dolphin film, when we had one of the scientists riding toward us on her bicycle, there was a moment when she looked very uncertain as to what it is she was supposed to do. It was just a little look in the eyes, very subtle. In 35mm, it would be fine; you wouldn't really detect it. But in IMAX it kind of ruins that part of the shot.

SBK: When it's eight stories tall or whatever. How tall are they?

SJ: Well, they're six stories or eight stories. It depends. But they're real big.

SBK: When you said that IMAX films are sort of in between features and documentaries, what did you mean?

SJ: One way that IMAX films are a hybrid is in terms of the visual format. We use a style of photography that is sort of halfway in between. We can't get by with a shaky handheld thing that looks really neat in 16mm and plays great on television and gives you a sense of being there, and which we all really like. If you use that same technique in IMAX, what you get is a bunch of jumbling . . . you just have to close your eyes . . . you can't accept that.

So photographically, we lean toward the smoothness of moves that are used in feature films. In fact, when it comes to aerial photography, there are shots that are acceptable for features that are unacceptable in IMAX, because we require even smoother, more technically perfect images than features, because a jittery aerial in IMAX is something that's unwatchable. On the other hand, there is a documentary flavor to the scenes in IMAX that feature films don't have. Some of the ways that people act is much closer to a documentary than it is to a feature. So in that sense it's a hybrid.

In terms of the storytelling, we try to use some feature film techniques because the films are relatively short—forty minutes—so you want to try to hone your story before you go in. We can't afford to just shoot miles and miles of footage, so we're thinking in terms of our script going in. Of course, we change the script based on events and unanticipated things that happen during production, but we have more of a plan going in than you would normally have on a documentary. We actually script the films before shooting. So in that sense, it's a little bit closer to a feature, because we're trying to figure out what's the arc of the story, what's the beginning, middle, and end, before we go shoot.

SBK: So when did you bring Tim in on this project?

SJ: Very early. Basically, I wrote a treatment that was very detailed, almost a shot-by-shot treatment. We sent that up to Tim in Montana, and he turned that into a first draft. That's before we ever went to Nepal—just prepping in the early stages.

SBK: About how long before the actual climb?

SJ: We went in March of '96, and this would have been in the fall of '95.

SBK: Now, you said you're not a climber?

SJ: No, I'm not a climber. Never will be.

SBK: What kind of background work did you do to know about what kind of story you might be able to get?

SJ: We talked a lot to David Breashears, who's filmed there a lot and knows what the angles are. Having shot in the Khumbu region and on Everest, he's thinking, "I know where I can get good shots." David's a very, very skilled climber. He's the first American to summit Everest twice. He's the first one ever to transmit live video images from the summit of Everest. And he is the "go to" guy as far as getting images on Everest—the most experienced and an extremely gifted climber.

SBK: Had you worked with him before, or you just knew of him?

SJ: No, we'd never worked with him, and Greg [MacGillivray] was trying to find the right person to do this. Greg's the one who was initiating this project and whose dream it was to do this. He heard a lot of people tell him that it was impossible—that it was a great idea but it was impossible to do, for technical reasons having to do with the camera and the cold and everything else, but also just the sheer difficulty of filming on Everest and moving up there, much less making a movie while you're trying to get around. So he had to find just the right person to do it, and David Breashears was that person. And, really, without finding him, I don't know, maybe the film never would have happened. But once we found David, Greg is the most experienced of the large-format producers, and David is the most experienced of the Everest filmmakers, so it was a great combination, you see.

SBK: Was it David who created the camera?

SJ: The IMAX corporation has a really great technical division up in Sheridan Park, in Canada, and they did the work. They worked with guidance from David, and Greg underwrote the cost of having that camera made, but it was the guys up in Sheridan Park—Kevin Kowalchuk and others—who took an existing IMAX camera that weighed about 84 pounds and cut the weight in half, and then made it cold-ready so that it would operate at 40 degrees below zero. They used special lubricants so it wouldn't bind up in the cold, and they added a special crank so that David and Robert, when they were up on the mountain, could hand crank the camera and get it going. David was adamant that he didn't want some system that would rely on heaters, because he felt that that was not a practical way to do it. They actually set it up in cold chambers—you know, meat lockers—so that Breashears went in there and tested the camera in a meat locker at 40 below.

SBK: So in the fall of '95, as you were putting this together, what did your treatment look like?

SJ: I wonder if I have it. These are all old drafts of the script here. I leave them there to remind Greg how much work it is to write one of these films. [Laughs.]

SBK: So you'd already assembled everybody probably long before this.

SJ: Yeah. In terms of the team, we knew who the team was. I wasn't very involved in selecting them. Breashears knew most of the people except for Sumiyo [Tsuzuki]. He knew Ed Viesturs very well, and he had met Araceli [Segarra] and Jamling [Tenzing Norgay].

We also have a wonderful physiology advisor in Vermont; he's sort of the dean of high altitude physiology. He's a former professor at Columbia University Medical School and has done a number of physiology experiments on Everest. And we had geologists in Colorado and Boston and places, and gathered what we needed that way.

SBK: So this is what you sent to Tim, and Tim turned it into a preliminary script, not knowing exactly what you were going to come back with?

SJ: Um-hm. Should I call him up and he can tell you?

[Steve dials.]

SJ: Tim? Hi, it's Steve. I'm going to put you on speakerphone. . . .

SBK: Hi, Tim. Steve handed me a copy of the treatment he sent you way back in the beginning of this project.

TIM CAHILL: [Laughs heartily.] Boy, the movie isn't anything like that treatment, is it, Steve?

SBK: So are you saying you encountered surprises in between?

TC: Yeah. Major surprises.

SBK: Well, I first knew about this project from reading Jon Krakauer's book [Into Thin Air], *in which he treats the IMAX team as heroes, basically.*

TC: And they were!

SJ: We're very proud of them.

TC: We're proud of them and proud of being associated with the project, where these guys—not only did they climb to the top of the mountain, but they did the right thing morally. Do you remember that movie that was kind of a cult classic from the late '60s called *Medium Cool*?

SJ: It's a film that Haskell Wexler did.

TC: Yeah. It's about journalism, and in one spot they film this turtle. It's going the wrong way on the beach, and it's going into the desert instead of back into the ocean. It's going to die. And the question is: after they filmed it, did somebody stop and put the turtle back into the ocean? What is the journalist's function—to be the camera eye and watch people die and get that on film, or does a different kind of humanity enter into it? And I think that's what our guys were faced with in this thing. And to my way of thinking, they did the right thing.

SBK: Absolutely.

TC: It made it more difficult for Steve and me, but they did the right thing.

SBK: Where were you, Tim, when they were actually doing the climb? I know Steve was at Base Camp.

TC: I was here in Montana, but I was getting information coming in on the fax machine and by e-mail [from Base Camp], so I knew almost immediately that our team was okay, but Krakauer is a friend and colleague at _Outside_, and it took twelve hours before I found out that he was okay.

SBK: Steve, what were you doing during the actual ascent itself, when you were at Base Camp?

TC: Coughing a lot!

SJ: Yeah, I developed something called the Khumbu cough, as did a number of our expedition, because I had a problem the day I arrived at Base Camp. As I got up about 16,000 feet, I started to get dizzy and I sort of turned green and I couldn't decide whether my feet were really my feet. The next morning I was okay, except I had developed this Khumbu cough. I was scheduled to stay there only a couple of weeks at Base Camp, so I had left before the tragedy happened, and was back here in California.

TC: The Khumbu cough . . . people literally crack their ribs coughing. It's very common for people to get that up there.

SBK: So what were your considerations, Tim, when you were turning all this into a script beforehand?

TC: I think one of the things that Steve and the rest of the crew at MacGillivray were looking to me for is that I have had a lot of experience in the outdoor adventure sort of thing, and I actually have some of my own much more modest mountaineering feats under my belt. So they were looking to be sure that I could spot the kind of mountaineering clichés that abound. For instance, not everybody has an epiphany on the summit. As a matter of fact, when you get to the summit, you're mentally and physically exhausted. And to say, "Once I reached the summit, I realized that blah blah blah" is probably phony. One of the things I find happening over and over in mountaineering stories and mountaineering books is the false epiphany on the summit. So we watched out for those kinds of things. That was part of my job.

SBK: So how do you decide how to tell this story?

SJ: It's a complicated process, and it happens over a period of many months. We decide one thing before production, knowing full well that things are going to arise that will throw our script straight out the window, but we still give it our best shot to provide a blueprint prior to production. Then once we see our footage, I'll start editing it together, and the question then becomes, "How do you tell a story with the existing footage?"

TC: Yeah, it's a very strange process. Because IMAX setups are so difficult, and especially on a place like Mt. Everest, because the film is so expensive, the filmmakers want a complete blueprint of every shot they're going to shoot before they go. Therefore you write an entire script. How'd we do that? Well, we asked David Breashears, who's been up the mountain and spent twenty years around the mountain, "What's going to happen here?" "How are people going to feel here?" "Where are you going to be able to set up the camera and what shots are you going to be able to get?"

So I'd say something to Breashears like, "Maybe when you get to the top of Lhotse Face, you're going to be a little bit too tired to shoot, but when you come back down, can we pick up some shots here?" And he said, "No, we can't." I said, "Well, why not?" He said, "Because I won't be able to stop anybody, and I'm not going to stop. Once you're at the summit of that mountain and you're going down, there is emotionally no way you can stop them."

So we knew that. We knew as David got to the summit, there were fewer and fewer shots, fewer and fewer places to set up the camera, and we pretty much knew what those shots were going to be. We wrote down what the people's feelings and such were likely to be, but naturally we had no inkling that there was going to be this enormous tragedy and loss of life, so of course everything—everything—had to be changed. We then ended up working with what we had.

SBK: You were talking about the unexpected—coming back with different shots than you had anticipated. So just out of my own curiosity, how did they get the shot of the avalanche?

SJ: The avalanche had to be triggered. You know, you can't just set up the camera and wait for weeks for an avalanche to come, so it had to be triggered. But we also had prepared ahead of time a very thick plate steel box with a glass port with very thick optical glass, into which we put the IMAX camera, and it was operated by remote.

SBK: How did you trigger the avalanche?

SJ: With explosives.

TC: Just like they do at any ski resort. At a ski resort, if you get there very early in the morning, the ski patrol will be setting off avalanches with explosives . . . so that the skiers who've paid for a day of skiing don't get caught in an avalanche and die.

SBK: So it was above Base Camp, I'm guessing, where they did the avalanche?

SJ: No, it was nowhere near there, actually.

TC: Because we didn't think that we could catch an avalanche, and because avalanches happen every day at Base Camp, we had video cameras up there. We were going to try to catch things with video cameras that you couldn't catch with an IMAX setup, but when you think about it, you probably want to see an avalanche in IMAX.

SBK: So where did you shoot the avalanche?

SJ: Here. In the United States, in Colorado, and Utah.

SBK: But it's similar to what you experienced there on Everest every day?

SJ: Yeah, it's the same type of avalanche. You hear them constantly in Base Camp. And usually you have time to run out of the tent and see it, but it's nothing that we could have set up [to shoot] because you're ringed by the mountains, and you never know where it's going to happen. . . .

TC: Part of the thing that wasn't in the film is that a year previous, in 1995, Araceli, one of the climbers in the film, lost a good friend in an avalanche on Everest. So it's a constant danger there.

SJ: Originally we had worked it in with Araceli's story, because that was a real factor for her; it was a very close friend of hers who died. But it was actually too personal, and she didn't want us to go into that, and that's why we took that element out of the story.

SBK: So we get her story about chocolate, but not . . . I understand that, though.

TC: Well, I have to tell you, we are dealing with people who are extremely strong-willed people. You have to have a lot of will to get to the top of that mountain, and believe me, once they get down from the mountain, you do not put words in their mouth. They do not say things that they don't believe or don't want to say.

SBK: Did you interview them before the trip?

SJ: I didn't. We interviewed them after the expedition.

TC: No, but I talked with Ed and Paula [Viesturs, Ed's wife] ahead of time.

SBK: A quick factual question: How much does it cost per minute of IMAX film?

SJ: I guess it's about a thousand dollars a minute.

SBK: Once they got back with the film, did you and Tim gather together here in the editing room?

SJ: We should explain our ping-pong method. Tim and I don't sit down at the same time and like, "Okay, now we're going to be cowriters." It's more a matter of I'm piecing together the footage, and I just record whatever the previous draft was, and I'll lay that in, and change this and change that, and then at a certain point we'll make a video, and Tim won't have been involved in that part.

Then I'll send him the video and the draft, or sometimes he'll come down here, and he'll take over the writing and I'll step back and supply ideas, but he'll be given free rein.

SBK: Once you had all this footage and you had this tragedy that you were dealing with and you had to rewrite and rethink through . . .

TC: The tragedy was extremely difficult. We could have done an entire film on the sheer logistics of what happened and why. But the pure fact of the matter was that our filmmakers weren't on the mountain with those people, so we didn't have that footage. And secondly, our thought was that our team had triumphed—both physically in that they had made the summit of the mountain, which was their original goal, and morally, by putting down their cameras and allowing the rescue workers to use all their oxygen, which was stowed high on the mountain, to aid in saving lives. So what we ended up doing was making a film that includes the tragedy—about a quarter of the film, I think, deals with the tragedy—but the remaining three-quarters of the film are about our team's triumph.

SJ: It was very important for us not to tell the story of the tragedy—not to try to do *Into Thin Air* in IMAX. What we were doing was telling our own team's experience of the tragedy, and it helped a lot when we focused in on Ed and made it "this is Ed's experience of the tragedy." It was very much a personal moment and experience that he had, and it was also true that we couldn't make it work until we were willing to give up certain things. Obviously from different accounts we knew a lot about what went on. And Scott Fischer was a very important figure in everything that happened up there on the mountain, and we tried every which way to include him in our telling of the tragedy, and it never worked. We wanted to pay tribute to Scott, but it was only when we were willing to give that up that we could make a coherent story within the context of our whole movie.

I think finally it was a matter of partly me looking at the shortage of images as working to our benefit. Ultimately I tried to treat that section of the film visually as a very abstract montage—there are shots of the moon, there are shots of clouds, there are shots of mountains, there are shots of blowing snow, there are still photographs. A lot of times you're not seeing what we're talking about. And once I looked at that as a benefit, because it allowed the sequence to be more emotional, then I could work with it. But when I first approached this whole sequence of the tragedy, the lack of images was a problem for me.

TC: Yeah, that was one of the hardest things. Steve put that together brilliantly, actually. But God, we tried so many ways of doing it.

SBK: So now, Tim, after you've done Everest *and* The Living Sea *and the kayaking movie, as well . . . when you're back writing a plain old travel piece, it's not boring or anything, is it?*

TC: Oh, no. I have probably the best job in American journalism. I go out wherever I want to go in the world, write just about whatever I want to write about. I love the work.

SBK: So your own life, is it pretty much made up of a balance of lots of different projects—your column and books as well as movies?

TC: Yeah, I have a book about Africa—a trek across the Congo basin that I'm writing. I have a monthly column to write for *Outside*, which keeps me pretty busy, because they want me to be somewhere strange and remote in the world every month, so I'm recently back from South Africa, where we were watching ignorant people swim with sharks, and I'm afraid I was one of those ignorant people.

SBK: Wait. Ignorant people do what?

TC: Get in the water with great white sharks.

SBK: You actually got in the water?

TC: Well, they're caged.

SBK: So is there anything you won't do?

TC: [Laughs.] Well, I probably won't climb Mt. Everest.

A Conversation with . . .

Roberto Benigni

For some, it might have seemed the most improbable job, if not impossible: to craft a movie about a father's love, and how a father's playfulness and ability to weave a story saves his child in a concentration camp. But for Roberto Benigni, writer, actor, director, and one of Italy's best-known and best-loved people in the movies, it was the supreme challenge, and one he wanted to do.

So one rainy day, in a café, he cooked up the idea and improvised some of the possible scenes to his cowriter, Vincenzo Cerami. The two ran with it for a year and a half, adding to it, giving it shape, before putting it down on paper as a first draft.

And when they put it down on paper, they had created a two-part story where Roberto Benigni, most often regarded as a man of comedy, ventures from careening through town in a runaway car, wooing his "principessa" (played by Nicoletta Braschi, Benigni's real-life wife), to an uncertain fate in a concentration camp.

But who better than a clown, suggests Benigni. "Because clowns, they are the image of purity. They are like kids. Innocents. They radiate gladness. So to imagine a clown going to die—the face, the body of a Charlie Chaplin or a Buster Keaton or Harry Langdon or Stan Laurel—in a very tragic situation, I start to cry immediately."

Benigni himself radiates gladness. He may profess a fondness for melancholy, but when you are in a room with him, he does, indeed radiate gladness. He talks with his hands, fishes occasionally for the English word or phrase, and smiles a lot—not the nervous kind of smile, but the kind that makes you want to smile and nod with him. As a boy, he worked as a magician's assistant, then as a street performer in Tuscany. By nineteen, he'd moved to Rome and begun working as a stand-up comedian and in experimental theatre, which led to a writing collaboration with Guiseppe Bertolucci, brother of Bernardo. And along the way he read. Lots. His talk is peppered with references to Dante, Schopenhauer, Gogol, Mark Twain. It's said, and he confirms, he wooed his wife by reading her stories of Isaac Bashevis Singer.

A few hours before *Life Is Beautiful* (La Vita e Bella) premiered in L.A., Roberto Benigni sat down and talked about the writing of the movie with Vincenzo Cerami.

SBK: Are you and Vincenzo Cerami writing partners? Did you write Life Is Beautiful *together?*

ROBERTO BENIGNI: Yes. I wrote with him my last four movies. Vincenzo Cerami is an Italian writer—very well known—a very dramatic writer.

SBK: When you first had the idea for this movie, what was it like in that room? What did you say to him?

RB: This is a good question. We were in a very, very melancholy restaurant in Rome. It was raining, and the restaurant was really very melancholy, which I like, to be in a melancholic place. And no good food, really—a terrible evening.

And we were thinking a lot of the time before we met . . . This is one of my favorite moments. The war is for real, but you can think what you want—the imagination—I can be in another universe; I can be an ant or a crocodile; I can be a Sicilian or an Alaskan. And during this moment, this idea came to me really naturally, without thinking, just free. I told him, "What if I try to improvise a monologue in order to protect my son, telling him this is a marvelous place—and this is an extermination camp?" And Vincenzo Cerami told me we have to stop and we have to think about it because he was very touched and very moved by this monologue. I improvised a very long monologue, trying to be happy, happy and funny in the extreme situation, because it couldn't be set in another place, because an extermination camp is not like Bosnia or like Cambodia. In our memory, extermination camps, they took the place of Dante's Hell. It's something not comparable, just unique. So it's tragedy.

So when I improvised this, Vincenzo told me we have to think about it. We didn't think about the love story, which is absolutely necessary for the movie. I couldn't shoot the movie two hours in a concentration camp, because I am a comedian. I am not the kind of director . . . Spielberg or Scorsese, they are the kind of director who can show violence directly. They can tell a different story. Moreover, I am not a documentarist, so I had to justify this love story. We needed it. As Dante said, "There is no greater sorrow than thinking back upon a happy time in misery."

So in the second part of the movie, the tragedy, we think about the first part, how happy we were. So it's more heartrending, you know. We needed to show an entire life. In the first part is the image of happiness, of freedom, of joy to live, something really full of gladness. We remember this entire life, when I am conquering her with miracles. And I am the same character, because I am using the imagination, the fantasy, as well, in the second part, in an extreme situation. I am the same character in a different situation.

SBK: When you wrote the very first draft of this script, did it include the love story?

RB: Yes, immediately, because we needed it. And I must say that the comedy, as usual, is always more difficult than tragedy. We spent a lot of time to write the first part, then the second part very less time, because comedy is always very, very, very difficult. There is no comparison, ever, between comedy and tragedy. Comedy is always more difficult and more tough. When we were working with Walter Matthau, he told me a story about a friend of his, I don't remember the name, who was dying. And [Matthau] was there and he told his friend, "It's hard to die." And he answered him, "It's hard as comedy."

Then the difficult thing was to balance the tragic, because in the second part there is, of course, the sensitivity of everybody. As Kandinsky said, "If I hear a joke about the Holocaust, I leave the town." It's impossible to make a comedy about the Holocaust. But a comedian making a movie, yes, because you can imagine a clown in a tragic situation. . . and when you have the script, you have the movie, because as René Clair said, "There are three important things in making a movie: the first one is the script, second the script, and the third the script."

SBK: Exactly. So what's so hard about writing comedy?

RB: It's so hard because in the first part of the movie there is the love story. It's a comedy—anything can happen. It can destroy the movie because it's full of gags, body gags, mixed with romantic. And it is very, very difficult to understand the style, because the style of the first part is the whole movie. Without the first part, the movie's dead. It's lost. Completely. The way I am conquering her—the character of Dora, Nicoletta Braschi—it's very difficult, because it has been done a thousand, thousand times. The story of the war, a love story, a man who is conquering a woman, no?

When I spent the night with her, this is the toughest moment, because I am telling her I love her, but I have to demonstrate with an *image* that I love her. There are a lot of movies they need to say to her a thousand times "I love you, I love you," because they don't demonstrate it. So they have to tell. And the audience, "Oh, he loves her, because he is telling her." But you don't need to say it. You have to feel it and demonstrate it with an image and with the script that you love her. This is really very, very difficult, and it's very rare—to watch a real love story where you can feel and you can see, not hear, "I love you." You can check a lot of movies, they are saying a lot of times, "I love you, I love you so deeply"—but why? Let me see why.

So the first part of the movie, there is such an amount of work—building the party, for example, the gag. And to put this dark sign, the dark sign of Fascism—the monster is coming, the monster is nearby—it wasn't so easy.

SBK: And it amplifies. It gets bigger and bigger and more and more undeniable.

RB: Right, and then the real tragedy comes. So we are funny, and then the real tragedy comes.

SBK: How many drafts of this did you do, you and your partner?

RB: Oh, three drafts. Just three. Because the first draft, we talked, and we talked so long, so much, me and Vincenzo, so the first draft is already almost the last. Before we started to write, it passed more than one year, one year and a half. So we talk and we talk and we talk, and then when we start to really write, it's done already. Then we do the second draft just for the rhythm, to change some dialogue here and there. And then the third, after some months, we read fresh—we need time to read and then we discover, "Oh, this is too much." But when we write, it's already done, the movie is there.

SBK: Almost everything that happens in the second half, we see set up in the first half—the riddles, the little boy. . . .

RB: The little boy, he doesn't like to have showers. And Ferruccio with Schopenhauer and the dog. There is a lot of metronymia, we call it. The interior rhyme. Where you put the seeds in the first part, and the flowers in the second part come back. And the doctor. And there are some other little things that come back during the movie. And the song, "The Contes of Hoffman," there is the same song. Me doing this before going to die and doing the first part to make my son happy, don't worry, so there is a lot of this interior rhyme. And to make them natural is very difficult.

This is what Alfred Hitchcock called the McGuffin. Sometimes in a movie you have to shoot in a very natural way and write, because if you discover this will come back, this is really very bad. In the old ancient movies, we can discover immediately, because they subline. There is someone putting a gun in a drawer, and then you know this drawer will be . . . [gestures as if opening the drawer]. So the way to do it is very naturally. You have to laugh in the moment, and you forget. Then when it comes back, this is very good.

SBK: The Schopenhauer is a good example of that, because he's with his friend, and he's willing him, and it's played for fun.

RB: Right. I use it in the theatre. So it's used there, and then, in a very tragic moment.

SBK: Oh, the dog.

RB: The dog is barking at him at a very tragic moment. Because there, if there is not Schopenhauer, I am lost. And it is a way, also, to remember Ferruccio, my friend, who disappeared.

SBK: So did you catch a lot of that way early on in your first draft? You planted those seeds in your first draft?

RB: Yes, because after one year and a half, we are talking about this, and in *Johnny Stecchino* there are a thousand of these, some very hidden. We have to watch the movie two times to discover all this, because there are a thousand of these, really.

SBK: How do you and and Vincenzo work together? Do you meet in a café or do you have an office?

RB: We change places. We go out of Rome in Tuscany or somewhere in a house and like monks, we stay there. On a couch like this, we take always the same place, very mechanically, because you think better in the same place—your thoughts are there. And then I start to play suddenly—and him, too. And I play all the characters—so I am just improvising monologue—and he is a very good narrator. So he is very good to build the structure, the structure of the tale is very important to me. I like to be free to improvise, and he is very good in the building, which is very, very important. Now we need something, we have to go in another direction. He knows about his job.

SBK: Do you work with a notepad or a computer?

RB: No. He uses a computer, not me. I have my little [notebook], like Chekhov could do.

SBK: I've heard about your notebook, your notebook with phrases and all, right?

RB: Right.

SBK: I heard also that about a dozen years ago, you did a short with Jim Jarmusch and Stephen Wright.

RB: You're right—*Coffee and Cigarettes*—about ten years ago.

SBK: Well, the thing about Stephen Wright . . . he's hysterically funny, but I would think his humor would be dependent upon the language. But you weren't quite so fluent in English ten years ago, and you still thought he was funny.

RB: Oh, I wasn't so funny with the language, because I couldn't talk in English. Neither now! But Stephen Wright is using the language in a way I never heard. I went to watch a show, and it was wonderful. Improvising questions from the audience. I didn't understand anything, but I could understand that he was great, really great.

SBK: How could you understand? I'm just curious.

RB: I understood he was great because his relationship with his work was amazing. Amazing. I was very proud to make this short, five minutes.

SBK: And was Jim Jarmusch working with you on it?

RB: Jim Jarmusch was there directing. And we just improvised. It was a joke—a very serious joke, but just a joke. So he directed and we tried it a lot of times before shooting it.

SBK: Getting back to Life Is Beautiful, *I think it would be a very tricky balance to walk with a subject that is so tragic. What were the things you had to rewrite or go back in and be extra careful of as you were writing? Do you remember some of those specifically?*

RB: Oh, yes. And we cut some scenes, because we needed in the first part to explain exactly why my friend and I, we are not twenty years old, we are about forty. So given we are there, but why? And to repeat that he is a poet, he wanted to edit, and me, I wanted to be a waiter, but I wanted to open a bookshop. So there were a lot of things to explain. And this is very dangerous when you are writing a script, because you are giving news. And if you don't find a way naturally to give news, that's terrible.

We can sometimes feel immediately: "So your father is a doctor and . . . ," and you explain because you don't find a way. There is such an amount of news in the first part of the movie to explain: who my uncle is and why we are there, what we are doing there. So we rewrote a lot of times the first part of the movie. And then I cut the scene with Ferruccio and an editor. And the death of Feruccio, we cut it also, in the concentration camp, because the story was between me and my son and my wife, and now if he came back it was old style, something commedia Italiana, very old. Everybody when he's writing has this kind of problem.

SBK: And also dealing with a sensitive subject.

RB: Oh, yes, a very sensitive subject. We did a lot of research about it and we had to stop sometimes because the details are unbearable, really unbearable. And we couldn't go ahead. But this is the kind of subject, of course, you must be very careful, but we loved so much the idea.

SBK: I know you did extensive research—read a lot and talked to a lot of people. . . .

RB: Survivors, yes . . .

SBK: What were you especially wanting to find out from them?

RB: Oh, because I was afraid . . . [I did not want] to be offensive or to hurt the memory of survivors. I respect so deeply this tragedy—it's impossible. But I sent the script to the Jewish community in Milano, and they helped me a lot with research, and survivors were with me, telling me a lot of things . . . the gas chamber, the concentration camp—they helped me a lot. But they knew. I had to give [myself] license, freedom, because I am not shooting a documentary in a concentration camp. It was a fiction story, a fable.

SBK: Was that your idea, to make sure that the movie opens with "This is a fable"?

RB: Yes, my idea, with Miramax. Harvey Weinstein. We decided to do this. Me, when I am watching the movie, I always say, "Oh, if I could retouch it, just to cut." But a movie is impossible. When it's edited, it's done. So when Harvey Weinstein told me, "Do you want to think about if there is something [you want to change]?" "I thank you," I told him, "because that's what I want—if you agree with me what to cut—just a question of rhythm, not ideology." The second part of the movie is exactly the same. The first part of the movie we cut seven, eight, nine minutes. And I put this voice-over which I wrote with Vincenzo Cerami. And I like it, and Harvey Weinstein, too. Because people understand immediately there is something dark inside the movie. Otherwise the passage is divided into parts too strong, but they like it this way. And it's moving when the voice-over comes back at the end.

SBK: In a way, this movie is an homage to storytelling and the power of the story, because for the boy, the father is trying to create a world by story.

RB: Oh, thank you. You're right. Nobody noticed that, and I thank you for that. Because it is also an homage to the storyteller. This is an homage to Mark Twain, to Gogol, to Shalom Aleichem, because the power of the storyteller is . . . You know, there is an anecdote, the Russian writer Nabokov, he wrote that he saw, one day, people were trying to pull out a big tree by the roots, and they weren't able to pull it out. Then one of them jumped on the tree and started to sing. And then with more weight, and a man less, they were able to pull it out. So this was very touching. The storyteller, the poets, and the artists are like this—they don't do anything—they are more weight—but they give the strength. Without them, we are not able to do anything. We don't have the music, we don't have the life, we don't see anything. So this is a wonderful story I remember very, very deeply, because it's a writer example. So it's an homage to the storyteller, which is the most ancient job of the world.

A CONVERSATION WITH . . .

Marc Norman and Tom Stoppard

A few facts about *Shakespeare in Love* and the men who wrote it:

- The movie did, indeed, begin with a phone call from Marc Norman's college-age son.
- It did take about ten years from that phone call till the time it hit the screens.
- Both writers are over thirty.
- Both writers are multigenre'd—Marc Norman's written screenplays, three novels, a musical (*Ormer Locklear*) which played at L.A.'s Taper Too, while Tom Stoppard has written for theatre, radio, television, and screen, and directed the film version of his play *Rosencrantz and Guildenstern Are Dead.*
- Both swear they are not Shakespearean scholars.

About Marc Norman, specifically: He has his M.A. in English from Berkeley. Along the way toward going for the Ph.D., he realized he didn't want to teach English, and came home to L.A. to see what he could find in the movie business. He made the rounds of the studio personnel offices, filling out applications. In the blank that said "Job applying for," he wrote "Producer." Universal called him back; offered him a job in their executive training program. What would it involve, he wanted to know. "Training to be an executive within our motion picture company," he was told. Yes, but what would he be doing? Their answer . . . "Delivering the mail."

He turned it down. Then a friend called him "shmuck" and told him that's where it all begins. He called Universal back, took the job, and found his coworkers in the mailroom were Walter Hill and Mike Medavoy.

When Roy Huggins was about to start the TV series *Run for Your Life,* Marc asked him if he could sign on as a P.A. Huggins said what he really needed was stories. Marc went home that night and came back the next day with a handful of story ideas, from which grew the first of the many scripts for both TV and film he's written since.

On the day both *The Hollywood Reporter* and *Daily Variety* came out with glowing reviews for *Shakespeare in Love,* Marc Norman sat in the Four Seasons and talked about the movie's beginnings and his own.

MARC NORMAN: It was a long time coming. But I'm very happy with the way it turned out, and I'm really happy with the way it's playing, because people seem to get it. There's something about it that's kind of like an elaborate joke that takes a long time to tell, and pays off at the end. And you worry that people won't get the joke, and people do. And that's great.

SBK: I understand it started with a phone call. What was it that your son said in that phone call?

MN: Well, the children of freelance writers—and I've had this confirmed by others I've run into—your kids very early on get the picture that they better come up with ideas for Dad or Mom because it's feathering their own nest; it's in their self-interest. My kids started coming up with movie ideas when they were real young. Usually the movie ideas were, you know, a monster comes from Venus and blows up New York. But as they got older, they got more sophisticated.

I have twin sons, Alex and Zack. Zack was at Boston University in theatre, taking an Elizabethan course. He called me from a phone booth on Commonwealth Avenue in the rain, and he said, "Here it is: Shakespeare just starting out in the Elizabethan theatre."

And I said, "It's brilliant." Actually I said, "It's fucking brilliant. But I have no idea what to do with it." And I didn't, for a couple of years. It took me a couple of years to really find my way into it. I had to work on other stuff, and I just kept coming back to it. Eventually the way I found into it was by looking at the one thing Shakespeare and I had in common—we don't have genius in common, we don't have poetry in common—but we were professional writers. And seeing him as a professional writer . . . I mean, I know all about that. I've done that for a long time. And I said to myself, "You have to assume that he had the same kind of life." And that was the beginning.

Once that happened, I began to think, if it's a comedy, he's frustrated. There's conflict. What's he conflicted over? Well, as a writer, he's been writing crap and he knows it. And maybe other people like it, but he doesn't. He's in development hell, really, and he needs to break out. He's looking for an idea, and ideas seem to have deserted him. In the meantime, he's contracted to write this crummy play, *Romeo and Ethel, the Pirate's Daughter*. We've all written *Romeo and Ethel, the Pirate's Daughter*! It's what you do when you have to do something and you don't have something you want to do.

And I thought, what if that turns into *Romeo and Juliet*? What if this crummy idea becomes brilliant because of what happens to him in the course of writing it? And that was kind of how we got into it.

SBK: That's great. Then how long did it take you to write that first draft?

MN: I got the idea from Zack in '88 and I wrote the first draft in '91. It almost got made in '92—it fell apart about three weeks before it went to shoot, and it went into limbo. The real hero of that story is Harvey Weinstein, because there was an enormous cost put against the picture in turnaround, and people wanted to make it, but nobody wanted to pay the tab. Harvey Weinstein stood up and wrote a check and believed in the movie, and I hope to heck it pays off for him.

SBK: I heard you were living next door to Ed Zwick when your son called.

MN: Ed Zwick's on my street. Actually, we had worked in the same building for a while, when he was doing *thirtysomething*, and we had worked on another project and pitched it. It didn't go, but we enjoyed the process of working together. So I came to him with *Shakespeare*, and at first he said, "I don't think so."

SBK: You're kidding.

MN: No. At first he said, "I don't think so. I don't get it." And then he came back to me a year later, and he said, "Remember that Shakespeare idea? Have you done anything with it?"

And I said, "Well, I've been thinking about it."

He said, "So have I, and I can't get it out of my mind. Let's see what we can do with it."

And I said, "Let's."

And we went to Universal with it, and I had no idea at that time what the picture was going to be about, so I did this great tapdance pitch, where I just got up on the table and tapdanced.

SBK: Literally on the table?

MN: No, no. But I didn't know what the picture was going to be about, and I had to pitch something. I'm proud of this, because it's kind of the high-water mark of my ability to bullshit people. I said, "You're twenty-four, you're married, you've got three kids, you've got a wife you don't like, you're living in a small town, you're working for your dad in his business which you hate, you're miserable. One night a traveling theatre troupe comes to town, you're watching the actors, and you think, 'I could do that.' And the next day you leave town and you go to the city and you become an actor. And," I said, "it's 1585, and you're Shakespeare, and it's Stratford-on-Avon."

And they said, "Okay."

That's really all I had, and none of that's in the movie. And we made the deal at Universal.

SBK: Did you have a working title for it back then?

MN: It's always been *Shakespeare in Love.* And it had to be a comedy. The great thing about *Romeo and Juliet*—you really can argue that it's Shakespeare's break-out play, because before *Romeo and Juliet*, he's written stuff that's kind of like what everybody else is doing. There's one good play in there. There's *Richard III.* But you can say he's copying Marlowe, because it's a Tamerlane [the hero of Christopher Marlowe's 1587 play, *Tamburlaine the Great]* kind of character. You can really argue that before *Romeo and Juliet,* he's just kind of one of the herd—good, but not Shakespeare. With *Romeo and Juliet,* he becomes Shakespeare.

And what he does is he breaks the rules. In those days, comedy was comedy, tragedy was tragedy. Comedy was about lovers getting married. Tragedy was about a guy daring the gods and he dies. *Romeo and Juliet* starts out as a comedy and ends up as a tragedy. It had to be really radical for its audience. It had to be a real striking bit of theatre. And it was a hit and it's been a hit ever since.

SBK: What kinds of things had you done before this?

MN: I had done a bunch of movies. *Shakespeare* is the first of the stuff I'm really proud of that's gotten made. There are about four or five scripts I've written over the years that have not gotten made that hopefully may have a better chance now with *Shakespeare.* But for the most part, it's been kind of meat and potatoes movie work—a credit here, a credit there. Doing some rewrite work, like I got a credit on *Cutthroat Island.*

SBK: So when did Stoppard come along on Shakespeare in Love?

MN: Stoppard came in early. I had written it as an American movie. The more we worked on it, the more it looked like it was going to be a British movie, for the most part. Maybe with one big American star, but shot in England, for sure, and with a lot of British actors. And Stoppard read it and said, "Can I work on it?" And how do you turn him down? He's great.

SBK: How did it get to him?

MN: He had a deal with Universal. He had a kind of open rewriting deal, so they ran it across him, and he said, "Sure."

SBK: And you said?

MN: "Sure." So he did a draft after me, and he put in some shamelessly broad in-jokes which worked great and the audience loves them.

SBK: What's an example?

<u>MN</u>: Oh, you know, there's the thing where Henslowe is saying, "The show must . . ." And Shakespeare says, "Yes? Go *on!*" And John Webster, the kid who's writing *The Duchess of Malfi* and feeding the rats to the cat . . . a lot of the in-jokes. Actually he put in a lot of the *Twelfth Night* references because my girl was called Belinda. He changed it to Viola, because he wanted to end it with *Twelfth Night*, which I think is a good idea.

But I never wanted the audience to need to know about Shakespeare in order to enjoy the movie. When I was writing it, I kept on kind of envisioning an inner-city kid watching the movie, and I kept on saying to myself, "Is he getting it?" If he's not getting it, you're doing something wrong and need to change it. I did not want it to be an elitist film, an academic film, in any way. Basically I wanted to knock Shakespeare off his pedestal and kick him around for a while and then restore him to his pedestal, hopefully with a better idea of why he belongs there. And that's, I think, working.

SBK: Yes. And people who are more familiar can go back a second time and find more references, like "a plague on both your houses." I assume there are many more of that kind of thing.

<u>MN</u>: There are a few. There's Hamlet's skull, and a few other things thrown around, right.

SBK: Are some of those things you found on subsequent drafts?

<u>MN</u>: Yeah. Stoppard did a lot of them. Stoppard enjoys that kind of humor. So it's very Stoppardian.

SBK: Did you meet with him at all?

<u>MN</u>: We talked. We didn't physically meet till the production, but we had some phone calls.

SBK: Is what we see on screen pretty much the way you had envisioned it?

<u>MN</u>: Yeah. It really is pretty close. There's a lot that's been cut out, but yeah, it was all there.

SBK: What kinds of things were cut out?

MN: Oh, some secondary characters, some of the theatre backstage in-jokes that I really liked. What I love about the Elizabethans is that they were inventing our business. They came up with it all—they came up with PR, they came up with stars, they came up with everything. When you're doing an historical piece, you cross your fingers and hope your research will give you your story. And in some ways, research did, and it was gratifying.

SBK: *What did you find out in the research?*

MN: Well, like the thing about *Romeo and Juliet* really being a turning point, and the status of the writer in Elizabethan theatre. I found something wonderful. I found a lawsuit that happened about ten years after *Romeo and Juliet*, between a writer and a company. He had an exclusive deal with the company, and the company was suing him because he'd been contracted to deliver three plays in a year, and he hadn't. They'd paid him advances and they wanted their money back. And his counter suit was, "Well, I couldn't deliver the plays because the theatre was closed down by the plague."

The company came back and said, "We don't care. You can't argue force majeure. It didn't stop you from writing." And they appended his contract to the lawsuit, and his contract said, "You'll be exclusive for a year, you've got to turn in three plays, you've got to be available to rewrite other plays that the company owns, you've got to be available to write intros and epilogues to other plays, you've got to be able to write jokes, material, and songs for other plays we own." And I said to my wife when I read this, "I signed this contract with Disney last year!" I mean, they invented the contracts; they invented everything.

SBK: *How has* Shakespeare in Love *changed the projects that you've done since?*

MN: Well, any performer knows that part of the trick of doing good work is getting the opportunity to do good work. Since *Shakespeare*, I'm just getting better opportunities. When you're a development writer, you're sometimes only as good as the project you're hired to write.

SBK: *Did the word get out, though, that you had written this script?*

MN: Yeah. The script's gotten around town, and it's done very well for me. It's baffled some people who can't quite figure out where it came from, and then I show them some other scripts, and hopefully they understand.

SBK: *They can't quite understand where it came from?*

MN: Well, if you look at my credits, it's not the most likely thing for a Shakespeare project to come out of them. But I guess I've had this secret life. I guess guys who write lots of screenplays often have a secret life in terms of the stuff that they've written that just doesn't get around town. And it often takes something like this to get a chance to expose the other stuff.

It's reasonable a person might make assumptions about Tom Stoppard and Shakespeare. After all, *Rosencrantz and Guildenstern* was his break-out play, making him a big name in both London and New York and earning him a Best Play Tony by the time he was thirty. He'd been a journalist before that.

Afterwards, he prolifically turned out plays—*The Real Inspector Hound, Travesties, Jumpers, The Real Thing, Arcadia,* and many more—gathering awards for many of them. And has done screen adaptations of many novels, including J.G. Ballard's *Empire of the Sun,* John LeCarre's *The Russia House,* E.L. Doctorow's *Billy Bathgate.*

But three things struck me while talking with Tom Stoppard. First, he never went to college, a fact which only served to make me question the value of a college education. And English is not his native language. He was born in Czechoslovakia, though his family moved to Singapore when he was four, and he doesn't remember speaking anything other than English. And he writes with a fountain pen—- a Mont Blanc given to him by a director twenty years ago. He doesn't know how to use a computer. He gives the Mont Blanc–written drafts to his secretary, who then enters them into her computer.

A fourth thing struck me, also. He is as eloquent with the language speaking off the cuff as he is in his scripts.

SBK: *So what is this love affair you've had with Shakespeare over the years?*

TOM STOPPARD: It started accidentally. My play *Rosencrantz and Guildenstern Are Dead* grew out of a conversation with my agent. Doesn't that sound like L.A.? We were driving back from one of the studios in London where, to use the local language, I was pitching something. It didn't get anywhere. And on the way back, I think we were talking about a production of *Hamlet* which we had seen recently—which was, in fact, Peter O'Toole's *Hamlet*. We're now talking about 1963 or something. You know, suggesting ideas to writers is a completely pointless exercise 99 times out of a 100. People think they've got a good idea for you because they know what you did before, but they don't know what you want to do next, and you don't know yourself. But on this occasion, he said, "You should do a play about Rosencrantz and Guildenstern," and I said, "That's a good idea." That's maybe the first and last time I've had that kind of response to people suggesting ideas!

I had seen Peter O'Toole play Hamlet as a very young actor at Bristol, where I was a reporter, and I used to write about the theatre occasionally. That was my first real exposure to Shakespeare. Then writing my play [*Rosencrantz and Guildenstern Are Dead*] really made me understand at least that play by Shakespeare pretty well. It wasn't that I then became infatuated with Shakespeare.

I don't consider myself now some kind of Shakespearean expert. I'm not. I'm an intermittent theatre-goer. I've seen, I guess, most of Shakespeare's plays and have read the rest now and again, but it's not an infatuation with Shakespeare, actually. And when this script turned up, if anything, it was a hurdle I had to get over, because my first reaction was, "Oh, please, don't think because I wrote a play about a Shakespeare play I'm suddenly up for Shakespeare projects!" If anything, the opposite was the case.

But I started reading Marc's screenplay, and the first scene I liked a lot. And then I got to something which I loved. You probably recall the first thing you see of Will Shakespeare in the movie is that he's practicing his signature, and I just loved that. So it turned me around. My attitude was turned around towards these 120 pages I'd been asked to read. And then I realized that Marc had had this foundational great idea, which was to write about Shakespeare not as a genius, but as a young writer trying to make his way and tumbling into beds and predicaments.

SBK: So then you decided to take it on?

TS: Yes. I had an arrangement at Universal where I was looking at what they had in development with a view to finding something for myself. It wasn't, by the way, reading scripts. It was books they'd bought the rights to and that kind of thing. This was a slightly unusual situation . . . but it wasn't the first time I had been asked to work from a screenplay, because I did that with *Brazil*. But the situation there was different, because the screenplay had been written by the director, Terry Gilliam, of course.

But Marc had had this fundamental idea of young Shakespeare in love, and particularly of young Shakespeare who has not been treated like a genius by everybody around him. And I suppose, perhaps because it was an English subject, they thought an English writer would be a good idea—somebody who lived in London and knew the London theatre and the in-jokes from the London theatre, that sort of thing.

SBK: What was the toughest part about this project for you?

TS: Well, getting into it at all. Because it's odd getting into somebody else's work. To tell you the truth, coming from the theatre, the situation even now strikes me as much more peculiar than it strikes anybody else, especially anybody else in this town. The idea of two writers on one film is odd in two different ways. In the first place, it's odd that it's not one writer. And looking at screen credits nowadays, generally, it's also odd that it's only two.

SBK: I know. You don't have this problem when you're doing plays.

TS: I don't. And furthermore, it would seem very weird if somebody gave me a stage play and said, "I want to do this stage play, but not in this form. It needs developing in a certain direction, or two writers are better than one, so have a go." All that would seem bizarre in the theatre, and I can't quite get used to it, even now.

You've just spent an hour with Marc, whom I'd never met before this movie, and who is very amiable about everything, and I don't know how he truly feels about everything. Because we're not the "ampersand" team.

SBK: Right. You didn't sit in a room and collaborate on this.

TS: We are the "and." As a matter of fact, of course, there are two-and-a-half writers, because the "and" is John Madden [the director]. You can't make a film without the director influencing the script, sometimes to a much greater degree than this one.

SBK: So what were some of your considerations, knowing that this was somebody else's script?

TS: I had to get past that and have none. And I don't actually recall the original script very clearly, because this isn't a recent event, you know. I think you know that this film has had quite a long history.

SBK: Yes. Almost a decade, actually.

TS: I didn't know it was that long.

SBK: Well, from the time Marc's son called him with the idea.

TS: Oh, it was his son! Why isn't his name on the movie, then? "From an original idea by Marc Norman's son"! Oh, I wish we'd had that. The Writers Guild could work that one out, surely. Oh, good. Well, look. I knew about it I guess five years ago.

SBK: In this rewrite that you were then doing, did you have to go back and do some research—Christopher Marlowe, for instance, or the other people?

TS: Yes, and there was something fortunate that happened. The archeological remains, the foundations of the original Rose Theatre, were discovered in London at that time.

SBK: In the '90s?

TS: Yeah, the early '90s. They were digging up the ground to put in an office building south of the Thames, and they found the original Rose Theatre under there. So it was really rather exciting. Then a woman wrote a book about the Rose Theatre just at that time. So I had the advantage of that going on. Not that it matters to the audience, I suppose, but the bare bones of the context of this movie are, broadly speaking, historically accurate. Ned Alleyn, played by Ben [Affleck], was indeed the leader of the Admiral's Men at the Rose Theatre. Henslowe was a real person who owned the theatre. Burbage was England's most famous actor, and he had his troupe at the Curtain Theatre across the river. All that was happening. And it's a lot of fun to invent inside the parameters of given historical fact. Christopher Marlowe did indeed get killed in a tavern brawl in that year. So, to some extent—not a major extent, but to some extent—the film is there to be enjoyed on an extra level by people who happen to know the historical context.

SBK: On a follow-up note, you've written so many plays and you've also written screenplays. What for you is the difference when you sit down to write a screenplay and a play?

TS: Certain differences are so clear that to speak about them is to speak of the truisms of the business. The arcs inside a stage play tend to be much longer. You can stay with the situation on and on and on and on. And even while I'm saying this, I realize it's only a convention and it's not true all the time. You can write a stage play which has an architecture much more similar to a movie script. It has been done. I don't think I've done it myself, really.

The whole question of what the audience sees, I think, finally dominates the writer's subconscious sense of what his job is, because a stage play is seen from top to bottom. I have no technical knowledge of these matters, but it's seen through one lens; essentially it's seen through a kind of wide shot. Therefore the disposition of the different points of energy in a scene are really up to the writer, because everybody gets to see the same wide shot. If there are three people in the scene, then it's a three shot.

With movies, you realize that the number of ways in which the scene can be manipulated by having this brought in too close or that brought in too close, this being off screen, this being on screen—the permutations are literally infinite, and they are under the control of the director. This is, I think, what lies behind the truism that in movies, the writer is there to serve the director. Whereas on the stage, broadly speaking, the director sees himself as somebody who's there to serve the text.

I think that there's a technical reason for this generality, and it has to do with the fact that plays take place in wide shots without cuts, so the writer has the responsibility of sustaining the tension or the interest in the scene. He has a much larger share of the responsibility. And because he's a writer, the burden lies heavily on the words. But even when that's said, inside every stagebound play there is cinema wildly signaling to be let out. And you can see this when you look back on your playgoing life and start recalling favorite moments, things which made a deep impression on you. Time and time again, there's nothing on the page to account for them. It turns out that these moments, these favored things, are not the utterance—they're something else. They involve a quite complex equation which includes what you're looking at.

A very good example of that just happened to me two nights ago in New York. I went to see a play called *Side Man* [by Warren Leight], and there's a scene in the second act which now has become quite a famous little moment, where three jazz musicians are simply listening to some jazz on a tape recorder. It probably lasts ninety seconds maybe, and it's completely riveting. Not a word is spoken. The little scene, if you can call it that, consists of the music and the men's faces and their body language, and that's it. So you can see that although theatre writing is thought of as being a branch of literature, that's not the end of the story. This particular form of literature has a lot of cinema in it, though, of course, that's a curious way of putting it.

And there's a paradox entailed in writing for the screen, I think. It's not built into the situation, it's just the way it works out. Because the energy of the narrative seems to be so important in movies, and because you know much of that energy is going to be carried by the camera, the words uttered—this is a kind of heresy, but—perhaps they are less important than other things. Or they have more to compete with, and so on.

So, here's the paradox: on the one hand, you feel that a lot of pretty good films have got away with something because they don't contain a single memorable line, and don't seem to need to contain a single memorable line, because that's not what they're for, but at the same time, I think those films do lack that very aspect. I know that's true because time and time again, when you're talking about films with people—you are telling each other the lines, recalling certain exchanges—there may be two or three in one movie. So what I said earlier about the memorable things not being on the page isn't wholly true. Famous lines do live on in the history of cinema, and I think that should remind us that, whatever else cinema is, when the truism has been dealt with, you still need to get back to the writer to make it an extra bit special.

SBK: I read somewhere that you said you make more from writing a good play than from your screenplays. Now we all know what the money is for a screenplay, and I would imagine you could get a lot for a screenplay, but you get even more for your plays?

TS: Actually, I wasn't saying that this is a general truth. I think I was defending myself from somebody who was assuming that I worked in film for the money. I just pointed out that it's not necessarily true that a film makes more money than a play. A successful play is capable of earning more money than any film script, but of course it takes longer to do it.

SBK: What was the impulse that led you to write your first play?

TS: The impulse was that everybody else was doing it. Anybody who wanted to be a writer in England in 1960 tended to look at the theatre. It was exciting and I think I wanted to be part of it. And I did write my first play in 1960.

SBK: Which was?

TS: It was called *Enter a Free Man*, and it's still around, actually.

SBK: And when was the moment, as you were writing, or whenever it was during that process, that you thought to yourself, "Hm—I think I've got it"?

TS: Oh, heavens. I don't think you ever think that. You have days when you think you've got it, and days when you know you haven't. And you just keep going.

SBK: Wow. Even now you have days that you think you haven't got it?

TS: Oh, of course. In fact, none of the plays I've written is entirely satisfactory to me. None of them. Not one.

SBK: Do you sit in the back of the theatre and rewrite as you're watching it?

TS: No, but I'm aware. I'm aware of something I might have done which I didn't do, or something which I did do which I ought not to have done, and so on. And that may not be because there's a platonic ideal, an ideal version of the play which you've failed to write. It's much more to do with the fact that the play's an organic beast, and it alters in relation to its time and place. So a play I wrote twenty-five years ago and probably seemed fine . . . you mentioned *The Real Thing*, and there's an aspect in that play which I would like to have altered, and in the case of a playwright, of course, you do get that opportunity, because it's not locked like a movie is. *The Real Thing* will be back in rehearsal in April, I believe—April or May—and I'll have another chance to mess with it.

SBK: Your plays are very intelligent, intellectual plays. Shakespeare in Love *is an intelligent script. But have you ever been on the receiving end of the comment that your work is too intellectual?*

TS: All the time. *Shakespeare in Love* has got a scattering of lines which exist on the screen in a simpler version than I would have liked to have had. I knew what they meant, John Madden knew what they meant, everybody knew what they meant. But there was this sort of general nervousness that out there are people who wouldn't quite get their minds around it if you put it in this form. And there's a scattering of lines in the movie which are just simpler than the line I wrote. Which is a good example of what I mean about the writer serving the director. For that matter, not just the director but the producers, too.

SBK: So from the time you wrote that first play till now, what do you think's the most useful thing you've learned about writing?

TS: Oh, dear. Not to try to figure out everything before you start. I mean, obviously you have to know what, in a general way, you're trying to write about. I'm talking about plays now, by the way. I think what I've learned is the more you plan, the less flexibility there is in the result. The less give, and the less life. If you can steel yourself just to blunder off into the dark and keep alert to the way it ought to go, then God will come to your aid.

SBK: So you make discoveries along the way, then.

TS: Absolutely.

SBK: Can you think of a specific time when you were working on a project, and you wanted it to go in one direction, and you were cognitively pushing it in one direction, and then you had this feeling that it needed to go elsewhere?

TS: It happens all the time. That's what I mean about not trying to get ahead of it. Letting it lead you, rather than push it forward.

SBK: Is there a time, say, with Arcadia *or some of your more recent scripts?*

TS: Yeah, there's a big plot turn in *Arcadia*, and I waited until I got to that page before I made the decision of how it would work. In the second act of *Arcadia*, two or three documents are produced which had been written one hundred eighty years earlier in this same house. I have a guy who shows up at this house and is speaking to a woman who is installed in this house, and I didn't know until that moment whether these documents were in the possession of the woman or the man. I didn't know whether she was going to show them to him, or whether they were in his briefcase as he walked through the door. I mean, that's a huge decision which affects the rest of the play—not just affects it, but controls it. Defines it. And I remember getting to this point and thinking, "What's best here?" I knew almost in a fraction of a second that from the point of view of the energy of the narrative, he should have brought them with him.

SBK: As you were at that moment writing it.

TS: As I got to that scene, I had to decide which way around it was going to be. Twenty years ago I would have planned everything, and even then, when I did plan everything, it went "wrong" as I was writing, and I was aware that you had to let it go "wrong" as you're writing. My sort of second play—I'm counting *Rosencrantz* as my first play—I figured out a first act curtain which turned out to be ten minutes from the end of the show. As I wrote my way along I realized I had a first act lasting two-and-a-half hours!

SBK: What would you say is the hardest part of writing for you nowadays?

TS: Well, movies and plays are so different.

SBK: How about plays first?

TS: With plays, it's inventing the story, because I always begin with something very abstract which doesn't involve characters or plot. I get turned on by the desire to explore an idea, something very abstract. So the hard part is to make decisions about who is saying these things to whom and where and when. So story is hard for me. Writing dialogue is neither hard nor easy; it's just something I do.

With movies, I think the hard part is to be economical. I'm not economical enough in screenplays. I have a tendency to deliver screenplays which are really plays with very short scenes, lots of very short scenes, which is not the same thing as a screenplay. And I think writing screenplays is a tremendous skill. When I read a good one, I can see what a skill it is, and I can also see that what I have isn't quite that. I have to work much harder to adopt the internal grammar of a screenplay.

I saw a movie just two or three weeks ago where there was a very nice scene. It ended with the actor stealing a glance at his watch, and that just buttoned the scene. The audience laughed, and you knew what he was feeling, and I sort of looked at myself and thought, "Oh, shit. I couldn't imagine myself sort of being there for that on the page and actually writing 'He steals a glance at his watch. Cut.'" I would have ended the scene with a last line of the dialogue. That's what I mean. It's a different way of thinking.

1999

A CONVERSATION WITH . . .

David Mamet

Some people are so well known they need only one name: Moses . . .
Madonna . . . Mamet.

David Mamet I first knew as the guy who wrote *American Buffalo,*
the most startling play I'd seen up till then, and *Sexual Perversity in
Chicago,* and *Duck Variations.* But he'd been writing plays for a
while, starting off at Goddard College in Vermont, where he took his
junior year to study at the Neighborhood Playhouse in New York and
gathered up friends like William H. Macy, and eventually moved
back to Chicago to become artistic director and playwright-in-resi-
dence at the Goodman Theatre. He'd cut his teeth as a kid in Chicago
working as a busboy at Second City, watching comics do their
sketches. His first play, *Camel,* written at Goddard, was an homage to
Second City.

Since then, actors have known him by dialogue so precisely rhyth-
mical they can't ad lib it. And audiences have known him by those
rhythms, as well. Think *Glengarry Glen Ross, Speed-the-Plow.* And
as he's written more plays and movies and television, his work has
become such a distinct part of the culture that entertainment
reporters and academics now commonly use his name as an adjective:
"Mamet-like," or as a genre of drama: "Mamet-speak."

So I went to the Bel Air Hotel to hear David Mamet speak. It was right before the opening of *The Winslow Boy,* and he sat by the pool as little children splashed, and he talked about that movie and iambic pentameter and "fuckin' Ruthie."

SBK: What compels you to write?

DAVID MAMET: I don't know. [Laughs.] I don't know anything about the process of writing.

SBK: You were a teacher of writing first, as I understand it?

DM: No. I tried teaching writing one time. Bob Brustein asked me to come to Yale and teach playwriting. I was a CBS Writing Fellow for a year at the Yale Drama School and was supposed to teach these guys about playwriting, but I realized I didn't know anything about playwriting, so I was a vast failure.

SBK: What didn't you know about writing at that point?

DM: I didn't know anything I could say about writing. It seems to be something that I can do once in a while, but I don't have very much either to say about it or I don't understand anything very much about the process.

SBK: What do you think is the best training for a writer?

DM: Well, writing. As boring as that is, or as formulaic, I don't know of any other training for a writer. Writing and reading. That's all that there is. There's nothing else.

SBK: Reading what?

DM: Reading everything. And/or reading whatever interests one. You know, my oldest kids are in school—they're fabulous students, straight-A students, and extraordinarily disciplined. And my heart bleeds for them because they're so smart and so interested; I think of all the things that they could be doing if they didn't have to go to school.

SBK: You mention in Writing in Restaurants *a fascination with two ideas you had learned as a student. One is that every aspect of the production should reflect the idea of the play, and that the purpose of the play is to bring to the stage the life of the soul. The first one is easier, so let me ask you about the second.*

<u>DM:</u> Stanislavski said that. That was what he said. So that's all it's good for.

<u>SBK:</u> *Meaning?*

<u>DM:</u> That's the higher level of the way to say a very closely allied idea, which is the purpose of the play is to amuse the audience, to entertain the audience. Perhaps the way in which these two ideas meet is by saying that what comes from the heart goes to the heart, if you have something very interesting to say, something important to say.

<u>SBK:</u> *In your daily work, how do you get to that place in your heart?*

<u>DM:</u> You know, the daily work is really a complete mystery. And I don't think there's any such thing as technique. I also frankly don't think (*a*) it's anybody's business and (*b*) that it's going to do anything, even if I were capable of formulating my thoughts sufficiently to communicate them to your readership. The question is how accurate would they be, and the second is, even if they were accurate, how helpful they would be. My generation was brought up being told that Hemingway wrote standing up. It took me many years to realize that perhaps this meant that if one wanted to be a better writer, one should go out and get hemorrhoids.

It doesn't make any difference. I think that there are people who are perhaps sufficiently driven that even a computer is not going to stop them from writing well. If you've got something to say and you want to say it by writing it down, you write it down. If you have something else to say and you continue writing, you're probably going to want to learn how to do it better, and you'll teach yourself how to write. And if those things are true, you will, and if those things aren't true, you won't. There's absolutely no mystery in it.

<u>SBK:</u> *One of the things that is distinctive about your work is your rhythms. I was listening to Dickie in* The Winslow Boy. . . .

<u>DM:</u> Well, that's Rattigan. That's Terrence Rattigan. I can't take any credit for that screenplay. It's rearranging the furniture in a Frank Lloyd Wright house.

SBK: You've said you love Rattigan. What is it you love about Rattigan and his work?

DM: He's a great writer. I've always been fascinated by the Victorian and the Edwardian. Rattigan's a terrific writer, and here we had a play which allowed me to indulge two yummy passions: one for Mr. Rattigan's work and the other for the Edwardian, and the idea of the British and the stiff upper lip and Mr. Kipling and all that yummy stuff.

SBK: It's also literature of the restraint.

DM: Absolutely.

SBK: I can't remember the line the father says, but he's asked, basically, "How're things?" "Everything's fine. Couldn't be better," when you know it's entirely opposite.

DM: Sure. And I think I responded to the play for the same reason that the audiences respond to it, because it's exactly the counter of the culture of self-indulgence and victimhood and thank-God-everything-is-terrible-because-I-can-blame-someone. It's extraordinarily refreshing.

SBK: Plus it's all wrapped around a kernel of ambiguity. I don't really know whether the boy was guilty or not. Do you know?

DM: It's very interesting you ask the question, because there is no boy, you know. It's a fiction. And I always thought this was one of the highest forms of compliment, to be sufficiently interested in the work of fiction that one wanted to fantasize about what happened when the characters went home.

SBK: So do you think it's important to know what came before? Did he really steal the postal note?

DM: It's a story, you know. People in Hollywood talk a lot about back-story, which is a very useful idea because it allows a lot of unemployable people to earn their living saying things to writers. It doesn't make any difference. All that we care about as an audience is what happens when the curtain goes up.

SBK: Do you write in longhand?

DM: Yeah.

SBK: What does it sound like when you're in the room? Do you talk out loud when you're doing your pieces?

DM: I don't know. . . You know, Lindbergh was an airmail pilot. That's what he did. He was a great, great pilot. Basically he was a blue collar guy who flew airmail, and he was awfully good at it. He became famous because he made a very famous flight, and his interest was not in the theory of aerodynamicity. He was a guy who knew how to get the mail from one place to another, and that was it.

And when Joey Mantegna and me and Denny Franz and Billy Macy and Lonnie Smith and John Heard and John Malkovich and all those guys were in Chicago, the theatre was, and is, considered a popular entertainment. It was very close to a blue collar amusement, like going to see the Cubs. It wasn't considered the realm of the academic or the realm of the self-referential. So we were very, very fortunate in having escaped the taint of intellectuality. We used to put on plays, and if people were pleased, that meant that we didn't have to drive a cab the next week, 'cause we could put on another play.

SBK: When you did the adaptation of the Rattigan play, what all was involved in that?

DM: Oh, a little bit of cutting, a little bit of rearranging, a little bit of writing.

SBK: Rebecca Pidgeon said you write in iambic pentameter.

DM: Sometimes.

SBK: As did Shakespeare sometimes, as do we all, sometimes, speak in it.

DM: That's why we write in it. It's not the other way around. Rudolph Arnheim wrote a wonderful book, a bunch of books, about visual perception. In one of them he said that the forms in which we compose the golden mean which gives us one-three-three and also gives us the Parthenon recapitulates the way that we see when we close our eyes. . . . And just so, as you say, iambic pentameter recapitulates a very, very natural rhythm of English speech.

SBK: Is it a deliberate thing that you do, because your writing seems so deliberate?

DM: Sometimes. Sometimes. Some people you just do it. I was just thinking yesterday, Yeats says, "The best lack all conviction, while the worst are full of passionate intensity." Those are two of the greatest lines that anyone has ever written and the most perfect examples of iambic pentameter.

SBK: I remember when I saw American Buffalo *the first time and heard Teach's "Fuckin' Ruthie, fuckin' Ruthie, fuckin' Ruthie, fuckin' Ruthie." People have been startled by what they've seen on stages for centuries, but do you remember what you were thinking when you wrote it?*

DM: Yeah, I was furious at Billy Macy. We had a theatre company—he and I and Stevie Shachter, who was out here directing and writing, and our third friend, Alaric Jans, who's a terrific composer and does the music for a lot of my movies, including *The Winslow Boy.* Those three guys were living in this little apartment and I was living at this hotel. None of us had any money, and I had come over to Macy's house 'cause there were three guys there, so it was three times as likely to have something to eat if one of them were working.

I opened the refrigerator and there was one little piece of cheese, and I took the cheese and I ate it. And Macy said extraordinarily sarcastically, and I will forgive him someday, he said, "Help yourself." I was so hurt—you know, being a sensitive soul—first I finished the cheese, then I slammed the refrigerator and I stormed out. I didn't speak to him for weeks. And I went back and I wrote this monologue about this guy who got ticked off 'cause his friend told him to go fuck himself 'cause he wanted a piece of cheese. That was that Teach monologue, which is the beginning of my writing that play.

SBK: Well, that solves that. When you did the screen adaptation of Glengarry Glen Ross, *you added only two scenes. Why and why those two scenes?*

DM: I don't know what the other scene is, but this one scene is the scene like something that I actually witnessed when I was working in the real estate business—the scene with Alec Baldwin. I always wanted to write that scene, and I think I very successfully resisted the urge to put it in the play, because it didn't belong in the play. But then I got another shot at it, so I wrote it for the movie.

SBK: Why did you think it didn't belong in the play?

DM: Because a play is like an airplane. You don't want to have any extra parts there.

SBK: But in a movie . . .

DM: A movie's more like a car; it can probably sustain a couple extra parts to make it look pretty.

SBK: When you went from writing plays to writing movies, how did that affect your writing?

DM: I was writing movies rather than writing plays. So, having been fortunate enough not to come from a theoretical background, the point to me was not how to use the soft currency of my playwriting expertise and make the movies eat it, but rather to learn how to write movies. I was also very fortunate that my first run-ins in the movie business happened because I was discovered by Bob Rafelson. He showed me a lot of movies; we watched them together and talked about how a movie is made.

Also I was very fortunate in that I had done a lot of reading, theoretical reading, specifically of the Russians—of Pudovkin and Evreinov and Eisenstein, and a lot of thinking about moviemaking.

SBK: What did you learn from them?

DM: That a movie is ideally a succession of uninflected shots which, when juxtaposed, create a third reality in the mind of the viewer such that when these third realities are added together they create a scene, and that similarly the scenes when cut together create the third reality in the mind of the viewer.

SBK: In your first screenplay [The Postman Always Rings Twice, *1981], what were the things you were working with to get right?*

DM: I can't remember. It was a long time ago. Trying to figure out what James Cain was trying to do and tell the story as best I could through pictures.

SBK: I heard you used to have a policy of not doing rewrites, and now you've done some. What changed your mind?

DM: I don't know that I had a policy. Maybe I did, but I think probably no one just ever asked me.

SBK: Now you've been asked and now you've done some. Has it been satisfactory?

DM: Sometimes. Sometimes not. But I think the deal is fairly plain. Jaye Presson Allen did something very, very nice to me years ago. I wrote a movie, *The Verdict,* and they didn't like the script. I got fired off the movie by Dick Zanuck and David Brown. And they fired me in a very polite way. They called me in and . . . I suppose they didn't fire me; I suppose I quit. They said, "We like the script very much, but it's really not what we had in mind. Would you mind writing it again? We'll pay your fee once again, but it's just not what we had in mind."

And I thought about it for a while, and I said, "I'm very flattered, but I can't write it again, 'cause I don't know what I'd do. I did the best job I could. I can't write it again."

So they said, "Well, then, unfortunately, we're going to have to get another writer." So they hired Jaye Presson Allen, and she was extraordinarily gracious. She called me up and she said, "Look, I like this screenplay a whole lot. I don't know what the hell I'm going to do to it. But they asked me to do it, and I'm going to take the job, and I just wanted you to know that I intended no disrespect."

And I thought, what a stunningly genteel thing to do. As it happened in that particular case, eventually Sid Lumet went back and shot my script, but I thought it was very, very nice of her.

SBK: When you're doing a draft of your own original script, like The Spanish Prisoner, *how long does it take you to get to that first draft and how close is that to what actually appears as a final draft?*

DM: It differs. Some scripts are easy to write and they kind of spring full-blown into one's head, and some scripts take a long, long time. . . . It's ultimately going to even out, and you do it till it's perfect. Or as perfect as you can make it.

SBK: And how do you know when it's as perfect as you can make it?

DM: Well, that's what they pay me for. And sometimes I'm wrong, too. Like I've had a long, long relationship with Art Linson, who in addition to being a producer is also a human being. One of the most objectionable things about him is that he has a great sense of dramaturgy. He'll look at something that I think is pretty damn good and he'll say, "Wait a second. Why is this here and why is this there?" And because he's my friend, I'll say, "Oh, you know what? You're right. Oh, golly gumdrops." Because how much better to figure it out before you shoot it rather than have to figure it out on the set, or figure it out in the editing room. I want to learn all the time, you know.

Sarah Green, a producer who's produced a lot of movies of mine including *The Winslow Boy*, taught me a great lesson. We were doing *The Winslow Boy*, and she did the board—you know, the day-by-day what do you shoot on each day. And she said, "You know what? I've boarded out a lot of these scenes, and if you look at them, several of them have the same log line—'Katherine meets Sir Robert' or 'Katherine and Sir Robert discuss the case'—there's two of them." She said, "I don't want to tell you how to write, but isn't it possible if the log line is the same, one of the scenes is superfluous?"

I said, "Oh, my God, that's the smartest thing I ever heard—give me back that script."

Because the ancient wisdom, which is true, is you get to write it three times: when you write it, when you direct it, when you edit it.

SBK: What do you like to get from an audience?

DM: I like 'em to enjoy the film. It's an arcade amusement; it's not penicillin. It's an arcade amusement—take people's minds off their troubles and give 'em a little bit of fun. And sell some popcorn. I was working on this play for a long time—this play about the universe and meaning and something—and I was talking to Macy about it, and he said, "You stupid motherfucker. I need to lock you in a room and show you the films of Preston Sturges." And I said, "You know, you're right."

SBK: What was it about Preston Sturges he wanted to show you?

DM: He's funny. I think he was thinking specifically of *Sullivan's Travels,* with Joel McCrea, who thinks he wants to save the world and he realizes the people want to laugh at Mickey Mouse. And I'm one of them.

SBK: What is it about writing that you haven't done yet that you would like to do?

DM: I want to do everything. It's always a challenge. I mean, it's always a challenge. That's what I love about it. It's always something new. I'm sure it's like fighting a war. You can't fight the last war, unless you're Henry Kissinger, you know. You've got to fight the next war. There's always something new to find out.

SBK: I want to ask you about copyright. In the Dramatists Guild, we keep our copyrights, but in the Writers Guild, we don't. Do you think it's possible to deal with the copyright issue at all, as a guild?

DM: Sure, it's possible. I mean, we're going to have much more luck dealing with the copyright issue rather than net points.

SBK: You've also written television.

DM: I wrote a lot of television, but I only got two things made. I wrote an episode and a half of *Hill Street.* Loved it. Of course, those were great people working on the show.

And then this woman called me up at CBS, and she said, "We love Dennis Franz." I said, "I love Dennis Franz, too. I've known him forever." She said, "We want you to write him a spin-off from *Hill Street Blues.*" So I said, "I'm thrilled." So I made up an idea and I told her and she said, "Great, great, great." So I wrote this pilot I really liked—I think it was one of the best things I ever wrote. And in the age-old Hollywood tradition, nobody called me up for a month. So I called her up and said, "What's the matter, you didn't like the script? Why didn't you just say so?" She said, "No, no, we love the script." I said, "What's the damn problem, then?" She said, "Well, as we think about it, we just don't think Dennis Franz can carry a television show."

SBK: And I guess that's been proven, week after week. [Laughs.] Would you like to write some more TV?

DM: I don't know. Like they always say, there's nothing harder in the world to get than easy money. I've been hired over the years to write so much television. None of it ever got made.

SBK: Why didn't it get made?

DM: Well, because people read it and some film school person says, "I don't get it," and so I, being somewhat gentlemanly, I hope, respond, "Why don't you go fuck yourself?" And there you have it.